Applied Spirituality

Applied Spirituality

A Spiritual Vision for the Dialogue of Religions

SWAMI AGNIVESH

HARPER element

First published (in hardback) in India in 2015 by Harper Element
An imprint of HarperCollins *Publishers*

P-ISBN: 978-93-5177-114-2
E-ISBN: 978-93-5177-115-9

2 4 6 8 10 9 7 5 3 1

HarperCollins *Publishers*
A-75, Sector 57, Noida, Uttar Pradesh 201301, India
1 London Bridge Street, London, SE1 9GF, United Kingdom
Hazelton Lanes, 55 Avenue Road, Suite 2900, Toronto, Ontario M5R 3L2
and 1995 Markham Road, Scarborough, Ontario M1B 5M8, Canada
25 Ryde Road, Pymble, Sydney, NSW 2073, Australia
195 Broadway, New York, NY 10007, USA

Typeset in 11/14 Dante MT Std by
R. Ajith Kumar

Printed and bound at
Thomson Press (India) Ltd

To

Swami Dayanand Saraswati,

who initiated interfaith dialogue in 1877

on the basis of the commonality among all our religions

in modern times for the progress of humanity.

God is Existence, Intelligence and Bliss.
God is Formless, Omnipotent, Just and Compassionate.
God is Unborn, Endless, Unchangeable and Unequalled.
God is the Support of All, the Lord of All.
God is Omnipresent, Immanent, Unaging and Immortal.
God is Fearless, Eternal, and Holy.
God is the Creator of the Universe.
God alone should be communed with.

— Swami Dayanand
in the 2nd principle of ARYA SAMAJ

Contents

PART I

1

Introduction

Human beings live in relationships; therefore, religion is essentially about one's relationship with the Divine. Every religion tries to enable the human being to relate to the divine and to the rest of creation, in a harmonious and mutually enriching fashion. It is from this perspective that the importance of religions and their interrelationship needs to be appreciated.

Alienation between religions, or relationships between religions marred by apathy or even mutual hostility, implies a contradiction of the very idea of religion. This is a reality that religions must come to terms with for their own salvation.

Religions are, or are meant to be, nurseries of the culture of hospitality, rather than fortresses of hostility. Hospitality implies the spiritual strength to accept the other in his otherness. The essence of hostility is the insistence that the other has to be a clone of oneself and, in the event of a refusal to change and acquiesce, the willingness to unleash violence to coerce the other into conformity. The great irony that stares us in the face here is that religions, which are meant to promote a culture of hospitality, have become hostile to each other, and in doing so, they have become contradictions of the very idea of religion. This is analogous to autotoxicity.

Every religion, in turning against other religions, is also turning viciously against itself. This underscores the need for religions that have been in a state of alienation and hostility, to work earnestly towards a wholesome relationship of constructive cooperation.

As with ideological differences, there are many reasons for this alienation: political and religious imperialism, the rise of secular materialism, and increasing consumerism, to name but a few. Further, a reductive Western ontology, more than any field of knowledge, has promoted the spread of deep-seated anxiety and hostility towards Eastern religions and religio-spiritual knowledge. This is because the Western world, in its belief in the supremacy of reason and materialism, has overlooked the Eastern philosophical-religious traditions, dismissing them as merely mystical.

The Western ontology of linearity insists on defining everything in terms of old and new, black and white, or progressive and orthodox, which connotes a neat opposition and polarity. This pattern is very much evident in the advent of the United States in Afghanistan and Iraq. A similar bias is also apparent in the Muslim reaction to the fundamentals of Western modernity. Both cases exemplify an attitude of animosity towards the unfamiliar and the alien.

Here, one can find religion entering the domain of power. When this happens, no religion can continue to exist in its pristine purity. Thus, it is necessary for religions to undergo periodic renewal, or succumb to the forces of degeneration and suffer a gradual demise. Throughout history, all religions have entered into collaborations with political forces in various ways and to varying degrees. For example, the spirit of triumphalism in the religion founded after Jesus Christ—who was as meek as a lamb—is a hybrid of biblical faith and Western colonial imperialism.

Triumphalism presupposes an arrogant unwillingness to know and value the 'other'. It conjures up the spurious need to conquer and assimilate other faiths. From this perspective, there seems hardly any possibility for interfaith dialogue. To a large extent, triumphalism still prevails in institutionalized religions; this contradicts the spiritual values upon which the religions are based.

In this context, it is pertinent to discuss the idea of spirituality vis-à-vis religion. One needs to be wary of the widespread tendency to equate religion with spirituality; they are, quite often, contrary to each other. This is certainly the case during periods of religious decay, like the present times.

Religious communities, like political parties, are crafted on the principle of sameness. Hence, they are marked by homogeneity. The foremost religious sin is heresy, which is, literally, claiming the right to choose for oneself. Thus, choosing for oneself is demonized and eradicated, not so much because God is too anaemic to stand it, but because this act questions uniformity and conformity. Indeed, what religions wish to root out as heresy might be understood, from an objective perspective, as the spirit of prophecy—the vocation to articulate the costly truth. Jesus of Nazareth was crucified because of this perennial problem in the theatre of religions. No prophet, he said, was accepted among his own people.

There is something insidious about this

conditioning through homogeneity and uniformity. It works in a subliminal fashion. Even freethinkers within a religious community, so long as they carry their religious labels, are not free seekers. The spiritual duty, however, is to *seek*. To seek is to go beyond familiar stereotypes. To seek is, in effect, to be subversive of the status quo. Seeking is the strategy for liberation. And the purpose of freedom is the pursuit of truth. Conversely, it is the pursuit (or seeking) of truth that makes us free. Truth and freedom are the two legs on which our humanity must move.

Moreover, religion tends to be oriented towards the profit and comfort of individuals. Personal salvation or the moksha of individuals becomes the foremost religious goal. This is not so in the case of spirituality. Spirituality is like an ever-expanding ripple; from the individual it spreads and embraces the world around. Spirituality integrates the salvation of the individual with the transformation of the society. That's why values such as love, truth, justice, compassion and so on are basic to spirituality. Spirituality emphasizes our shared destiny as a species, and not the metaphysical or material profit or loss that an individual might incur.

Contrary to popular belief, however, spirituality is profoundly this-worldly. But spirituality is this-worldly precisely because it has a true sense of the divine. This-worldliness sans godliness is the realm of materialism, but spirituality is godly materialism, to put it in another way. Quality of life as well as the health and wholeness of the whole of creation is basic to spirituality. This need not necessarily be the case with religions; indeed, it rarely has been.

This too has a material bearing on the interfaith movement. The Supermarkets of Salvation can only compete among themselves. Not so in the case of shared spirituality, which shifts our focus from the efficacy of individual salvation to the collective destiny of our species. In this process, the spirit of competition is replaced by the spirit of a shared sense of mission. Religious communities are formed on the contrived kinship of a comparatively small group of people; humankind is divided into *us* and *them*. In contrast, spiritual kinship involves the species as a whole, which is a necessary foundation for unity and universal oneness. The insight that we are all, despite our many religions, children of the same Creator God can only be a spiritual truth. In respect of religion, this is heresy.

The interfaith movement needs to be erected on the foundation of spirituality, not of institutionalized religion. Interfaith dialogue made little progress over the decades largely because it did not look at the horizon beyond religion that is common to all human beings and, therefore, to all religions: the horizon of shared spirituality. This failure resulted from the religious conditioning of the participants. Rather than seeking liberation through sharing, they ended up, more often than not, showcasing their religious wares or explaining away the aberrations that their religious community harbours.

Religious experience—and not exclusively the hegemonic power of institutionalized religion—needs to comprise the matrix of our interfaith encounters. We therefore need to come to some understanding as to what may constitute 'religious experience'. In order to facilitate some preliminary thinking on this subject, I propose the following features as mere markers of religious experience.

First, there is a need to engage the scriptures from a perspective of what the American sociologist Peter Berger calls the *heretical imperative*. Heretical imperative implies the duty to be heretical in the face of established and deeply entrenched dogmas that no longer square up with the truth of human experience. Our scriptures are a mixed bag. They contain much that is valuable and inspiring. But this great treasure is mixed up with suggestions and insinuations that are not very spiritual. The idea of holy war that, in some religious texts, sanctions the total elimination of a race is a case in point. The idea that God resides on a particular mountain (and nowhere else) and that those who cannot go there for worship must carry some soil from there for purposes of worship is another. The notion that the water of a river is sacred and can wash away your sin, or guarantee painless delivery for women, is yet another. The list is endless. Further, scriptures that denigrate the value of a human being on account of his or her faith or caste identity must be rejected. So should any false notion that the injustice meekly suffered in this world would be compensated in a hypothetical heaven. The idea of a partial God must be laughed out of court.

Second, the social isolation of religious communities must end. Sadly, the social distance between religious communities has only increased with the passage of time, and with the shrinking of the global village. Most regrettably, the rifts between religions have widened alarmingly in the wake of religion-based terrorism and the rise of belligerent and hegemonic ideologies. These legitimize themselves through deceptive religious pretensions and postures, underlying which is an unnatural state of being, promoted on purpose by vested interests. There is a need to reverse these trends and to multiply opportunities for promoting shared experiences.

Third, the escapist practices promoted by the priestly class must be critiqued and curtailed. Barring rare exceptions, priests in all religious traditions live in a state of isolation from social issues. Ironically, in their eagerness to see God they become blind: blind to the world around and to the world within. Religiosity segues into spiritual blindness! God is light. The function of light is to enable us to see and to respond. Because of our warped religiosity, we fail to see. We are blind even to the fact (known to infants and children) that the person beyond one's communal boundaries is also a human being. The religious wares showcased by the merchants of religions remain the same, irrespective of what happens in the world around them. The religious agenda is, more often than not, separated from worldly realities.

Spirituality is a clarion call to change in this respect. But the change called for is not one of fitting everything into a fixed framework. It is a change from what is, to what might well be—a change from the real to the ideal. Spirituality is a continual endeavour to bring out the best potential latent in every person or society.

At the core of the spirituality of engagement is the concern to bridge the gulf between religious knowledge and social action. It is not enough that we know. The spiritual task is to bridge the gulf between knowledge and action. Fundamental to this is the duty to draw together the self and the other. If our religiosity is robust enough to enable us to love our neighbours like ourselves, it will have a powerful and proactive social content. A passionate pursuit of social justice will necessarily be an ingredient of our spirituality, with compassion as its hallmark. Compassion is the ability to love others in deeds not less than in words.

God is the eternal Giver. The spiritual task is to become the conduit for the generosity of God. Generosity is not mere charity; charity, in its popular sense, is giving in a superfluous way. It is not only material resources that God gives. It is a comprehensive framework for total human well-being in a spiritually wholesome way. Applied spirituality, or the spirituality of engagement, cannot develop unless this shift from the self to the other—on account of being founded in God—is welcomed and internalized. The proof that we are in God is that we experience a passion for giving, of which forgiving is an innate and intimate part.

In the absence of the true manifestation of the power of God, the world has been filled with the demonstration of the power of man. This is true also in the domain of religion. In the gigantic structures and massive establishments we have built in the name of religion—purportedly according to the will of God—there is hardly any space for the expression of the will or values of God. God is an outsider, the Excluded One, vis-à-vis our edifices of organized and ritualized religiosity.

The first and foremost requirement to turn religion into an invitation to address the world around is to invite God to come into our spirituality. But God will not do so on our terms or fit into our narrow frameworks. Our religiosity is too narrow for God, whose presence fills the entire cosmos. Our pettiness is too mean for the majesty of God's sanctified sovereignty. The advent of God will hence be experienced as an explosion of heresy. We must have the spiritual robustness to withstand this religious trauma.

Spirituality is a sphere of ever-expanding responsibility. That is why it is also a medium of humankind's ongoing evolution. Spirituality is a vision that insists that one's welfare is coterminous with the welfare of the society. This is because spirituality presupposes a holistic vision, in which all the parts dwell organically within the whole and the whole dwells in the parts. One part cannot thrive at the expense of the other. As Jesus of Nazareth said, 'Whatever you do to the least of these, that you do to me.' Serving the poor, the excluded, the deprived, the exploited, the enslaved and the suffering is the surest way of serving God.

Engagement is the dynamic of liberation and empowerment. The tragedy with the prevailing popular idea of religion is that its goal is reduced to having rather than being. Getting some blessings or enjoying some privileges is a sufficient goal in the *having* mode of religiosity. But in the *being* mode of spirituality, the irreducible goal is the full unfolding of the potential and scope of our humanity. It is the empowerment to be fully human.

There is a serious problem in the *having* mode of religiosity, which today has attained epidemic proportions. If our relationship with God is driven by covetousness—no matter how pietistic—we debase ourselves; we become cosmic beggars. God is not a feudal lord, waiting to be flattered into indiscriminate favours or largesse. God is the Creator. The Creator is in a relationship of love and compassion with all that He has created. The foremost concern of the Creator is the authenticity of His/Her creation. A great artist will suffer heartache or be roused to anger if he sees a counterfeit of his work being sold as genuine. Beggarly religiosity—religiosity that reduces us to beggars in our relationship with God—makes us counterfeits of God's creation. It is in the nature of God to respond to His/Her creation. The substance and scope of that response is the zeal to safeguard the authenticity and integrity of the whole of creation. God is not sentimental. God is compassionate.

A commitment to authenticity is the hallmark of compassion. Such radical and proactive compassion cannot but have a social dimension. It breeds an irresistible urge—indeed, an imperative need—to engage the realities of this world and to reveal the justice of God in the midst of it all.

Spirituality of this kind has the power to liberate us from religious ghettoes. It dismantles barriers and enables inter-religious partnerships. This is essential to the liberation that spirituality affords.

The need for religions to shift from a relationship of competition to one of cooperation is being increasingly realized the world over. In no small part this is because religions have failed to impact the state of affairs in the world constructively, due to their mutual alienation and suspicion. While the custodians of religions busy themselves with their petty quarrels, the destiny of our species is being hijacked by the forces of ungodly economics and predatory politics. Our mutual quarrels have served only to marginalize religions.

When religions insulate themselves from the lived realities of the world, they tend to develop a purely other-worldly outlook that shuts its eyes to the issues that plague human existence in the given context and time. From such a disposition, religious rituals and prescriptions are employed only to secure the maximum advantage for oneself, or to manipulate the will of God to one's own benefit. It is with this logic that, under certain political and economic conditions, communalism and sectarian violence thrive.

This concept can only seem rather strange from the perspective of conventional religiosity. All religions have developed, one way or another, religious or doctrinal legitimizations for disowning their responsibilities to the world around. Some of the instruments in this respect are:

- **The idea of ritualistic pollution:** In several religious traditions, whatever is 'of the world' is treated as a source of spiritual pollution. Even contact with those outside of one's religious fold is coloured in this fashion. The idea of ritualistic pollution has been one of the most powerful instruments of interfaith and inter-caste alienation.

- **Fatalism:** The fatalistic world view discourages any initiative for improvement. The idea of a breakthrough even seems impious. This forestalls the possibility of forming interfaith partnerships to address social evils (cf. the attitude to poverty from a fatalistic standpoint, or the idea that if a person suffers it, it is of his/her fate).
- **The doctrine of sin and punishment:** This doctrine allows a convincing escape route from social action. Avoidable suffering can be explained away as the result of overt or covert sin, for which it is just punishment. So long as religion continues to be used as a means for legitimizing human suffering and organized exploitations in society, the idea of religion will remain suspect in the minds of those who dare to interrogate and to think for themselves.
- **The doctrine of reward after death:** Even when it is fully granted that there is a life after death—irrespective of the colour or shape that it might assume—it should in no way become an excuse for diluting the right of every human being to enjoy a decent quality of life and find the full development of his or her potential as a person, here and now. The extent to which the priestly

class exploits our ignorance of, and anxiety about, life after death is wholly condemnable. Often it seems that the idea of life after death is used as the opium to dull the pain of the life before death.

- **Exclusive emphasis on personal salvation:** As long as religions continue to operate only on the perspective of personal salvation, the scope for interfaith dialogue—or for promoting a universal, shared spiritual vision—will remain slender. Integral to the doctrine of personal salvation is the idea of exclusivity. All claims of religious exclusiveness hinge on the notion of personal salvation. This is the most formidable hurdle in the path of interfaith cooperation and dialogue.

The thrust in applied spirituality should be:

- **A spiritual idea of God:** The insult to God immanent in a communal or sectarian concept of God needs to be fully exposed. Rather than see the truth of the Divine as the invitation for personal and collective liberation and universal harmony, religious traditions caricature God as a partisan player in the market of petty-minded religiosity. All sectarian religions bear false witness to God. Their god is too small to reflect the spiritual splendour of the Universal God of all-embracing love and compassion. If God is recognized as the source of the human family as a whole, the petty quarrels between religions will at once look insufferably irreligious.

- **The ecumenical vision—a shift from exclusion to inclusion (cf. *vasudhaiva kutumbakam*):** All spiritually directed reform movements have fought against the walls and barriers between religions. The ecumenical vision is a mandate to see the unity of our species underlying its diversity and variety. It is based on the truth that creation itself is a harmony of the One and the many; of unity in diversity. While religious orthodoxy tends to be allergic to the plurality of religions, spiritual robustness revels in it and seeks to unveil the unity that underlies this richness and variety.
- **An incarnate spirituality:** It is distinct from disembodied piety that limits itself to the practice of rituals and traditions aimed only at personal salvation or moksha. The true nature of God and the authentic dynamic of spirituality as well as the depth of scriptures—all these become accessible to us, if at all, only in a state of dynamic engagement with the realities of the

world. Religions are not an anthology of magic formulae but manuals on life itself. Life does not lend itself to a dichotomy between the internal and the external. The reconciliation between the two and a dynamic flow between the two are basic to the logic of life. When this flow stops, the logic of death takes over, and death-oriented religions cannot enter into dialogues—for dialogue is a function and celebration of life.

- **A radical idea of worship:** It is not only a matter of going to have a date with God, but also an experience of equipping oneself to make the will of God (or godly values, such as justice, truth and compassion) prevail in the world. The flow towards the temple or church must be complemented by the flow from the temple into the society, to impact and transform societies. The temple / church / mosque as a symbol of one-way traffic (to which all must flow) is the very antithesis of the nature of God. It bears false witness to God and the very logic of life and nature.
- **A thorough revision of our self-images—and the images we entertain of each other:** The evil and questionable should not be ignored; on the contrary, they must be openly discussed. But we need a shift—a shift from seeing only ill in

other religions to exercising the freedom to see what is good and beautiful in them. Freedom is indeed the willingness to see what is good and valuable in everyone and everything. The inability to rejoice in the goodness of all that God has created is a sign of spiritual unfreedom. Freedom is born of love. Only in the light of love can others be known truly and justly. Such knowledge arises out of engaging each other with openness and humility. So far, religions have chosen to know each other from a distance. Knowing from distance yields, at best, superficial knowledge. Distance is a medium of distortion. It distorts knowledge. To know in love is to know at close quarters and without any prejudice. It is to know positively, rather than negatively. As long as the mindset of negativity is not removed from interfaith perceptions, the cause of dialogue will remain crippled.

- **Above all, a shift from profession and confession to practice:** Paying lip-service to spiritual values will not do. The emphasis must be on realizing and giving effect to them in the given social, political, economic and cultural context. Spirituality is a paradigm of engagement, and engagement is the dynamic of transformation. Applied spirituality must be seen essentially as a means for liberating religions from the enclaves of exclusion to which they have consigned themselves.

It is unlikely that a religion that is cocooned in its chosen shell and refuses to emerge will develop applied spirituality or a culture of cooperation. It is by disowning spirituality that religions ghettoize themselves. Conversely, only by developing spirituality can they liberate themselves. Throughout the history of religions, only those who saw the light of the *spirit* felt urged to come out of their religious caves into the broad light of shared spirituality. It is a pity, though, that most people still remain, thanks to their religious zeal, mere cavemen.

The basic dynamic of applied spirituality is the integration of the sacred sanctuary and the secular society. What connects the two is the river of love. We must go to our places of worship so that our hearts may be filled with God's love for the world. If and when this happens, we shall return to society and manifest that love through concrete actions. Unmanifested and unintegrated, applied spirituality is merely a new theological concept with a limited shelf life—yet another theological or academic fad.

When we return to the society and begin to engage its complex and demanding problems, we begin to see the limitations of the spurious religiosity that we have absolutized all the while. Until that happens, we shall mistake the shell for the kernel of religion. It is our virtual imprisonment in places of worship that has prevented us from developing our spiritual heritage, or claiming our freedom to be effective spiritual agents in our life-world.

Why should religions meet? Their meeting as a mere religious fad, or as a concession to this age of multifarious conferences, is a luxury we must readily forgo. Religions must meet, first of all, for their self-liberation. Second, there must be an emphasis on their revitalization as agents of social liberation and transformation. The focus here must be relentlessly on social justice. The competitive and isolationist models of religion have failed to bear witness to God's passion for justice in this world. Third, religions must meet and help each other in fulfilling their historic destiny as instruments for peace and human welfare. The ultimate spiritual goal is not to crowd the landscape with places of worship, but to turn the whole earth into one grand temple of God. The alternative to dialogue is destruction and holocaust.

The foremost spiritual task in the global village is to foster a sense of universal kinship among the peoples of the world. Unless the global village is inhabited by a global family, the chances of exploitation, coercion and conflicts can only increase. The nearness of religious cohorts will aggravate their mutual hostility, unless their closeness is tempered by a deepened sense of spiritual kinship. Religions should not be allowed to infect the emerging world order with the poison of alienation and hostility. The post–11 September scenario vis-à-vis Afghanistan needs to be seen as an early warning of the shape of things to come.

It is not enough to simply engage in dialogue. Dialogue of sincere depth must be a pilgrimage. It must be a mutual engagement which liberates and transforms the participants. Dialogue as the mere mouthing of shallow religious sentiments or showcasing of good intensions does not serve its purpose in the end. Rather than bypass or dodge areas of difference, the participants need to be engaged with open minds, with a view to deepening mutual trust and understanding.

Finally, dialogue must be seen as a spiritual tool, and not an end in itself. Dialogue for what? When this question is raised, it becomes clear that dialogue cannot any longer remain an esoteric exercise which some privileged people indulge in. It must become an integral part of our way of life.

For that, two dialogues need to happen concurrently. Our horizontal dialogue with each other must be directed by our vertical dialogue with God. Dialogue must not be a fringe activity, but a shared culture.

Overarching all of this is the need to shift from the dialogue of words to the dialogue of deeds. As long as our interfaith encounters are confined to the bandying of words, and our words and sentiments are not manifested through a shared sense of mission, the breakthrough we dream of cannot even begin to happen. This is as much a matter of personal integrity and commitment as it is of theology. The call with which the interfaith dialogue resounded for long, namely, to shift from orthodoxy to orthopraxis, is valid here. We must integrate correct words with creative deeds, and so unleash the spiritual power that would liberate the people and transform societies. Nothing less than this is acceptable as the goal of the interfaith movement for the third millennium.

2

Multi-faith Initiatives for Social Transformation: From Multi-faith-ism to Multi-faith Movement

Every institution needs to evolve with time, lest it begins to contradict itself. Institutionalized religion is no exception to this. When the original spiritual fervour of a religion dies down over time, it is superseded by the interests of the religious establishment. This facilitates the influx of worldliness into religion. Religion, which is meant to liberate people from the clutches of vested interests, becomes their playground and means of legitimization.

No religion is safe from this inner decay, and the pathology of religion can be seen both by what it does and by what it fails to do. Religion holds considerable spiritual resources for transforming individuals and societies. The goal of spirituality, in the Vedic tradition, is the ennoblement of all human beings. This calls for the creation of social, economic, political and cultural conditions conducive to such a goal. The Vedas offer a comprehensive, universal vision for humanity. Unfortunately, the ascendancy of Brahminical vested interests has distorted the pure light of the Vedas, which have been misinterpreted and degraded into an apology for caste domination.

In the Western context, and particularly since the dawn of modernity, the understanding and propagation of the biblical faith has been radically corrupted by the domination of power, resulting in the rejection of love as the shaping paradigm of Western culture. This summary rejection of the biblical culture was overlooked in the glare of power, control and wealth; the Way of Jesus Christ ceased to be the Way of the Cross. Biblical texts were deployed to cover up the nakedness of Western triumphalism and religious expansionism, resulting in the coinage of laughable slogans like *the Globe for Christ by* AD *2000, India for Christ by* AD *2000,* and so on. Ironically, these expansionist slogans began to emerge as the Western world ceased to be Christian. Midway through the nineteenth century, the European religious constituency was stung by Soren

Kierkegaard, the foremost Christian philosopher of the time, who lamented: 'Throughout the whole of Christendom, there is not a single Christian.' The more Europe ceased to be Christian, the more Europeans wanted the rest of the world to be Christian.

This obvious truth of modern history affords a basic insight. The conflictual model of inter-religious relationships is a product of religious degeneration. The foremost symptom of this degeneration is that the religious goal gets hijacked: from social justice and social transformation, they are co-opted into religious expansionism and politico-economic domination. The love of power (the hidden political motive) is incompatible with the power of love, which is the true religious outlook. Love alone has the potential to transform. The genius of power is in annexing and controlling. It lies in growing at the expense of others, especially of those who are similar.

This truth underlies the biblical story of Cain and Abel, in which brother killed brother. Fratricide (or rejection of kinship) has been the dominant note in inter-religious encounters throughout history. The source of all inter-religious as well as intra-religious conflicts is the truth that the warring parties are brethren. They are too similar in interests to live in peace with each other. In that sense, all inter-religious conflicts are, in point of fact, intra-religious conflicts, for there is only one religion—the religion driven by vested interests. This is obvious in the world of commerce and profit seeking. A shoe company will not be in competition with a pen company, but a shoe company could be in deadly combat with its rival shoe company. Religious companies are no different. Their trappings may differ, but the spirit that animates them is the same. False gods are false, no matter by what name you call them. They all belong together: to the domain of depraved human nature and the vested interests and hypocrisies it contrives.

INTER-RELIGIOUS MOVEMENT: A BRIEF CRITIQUE

Given this state of affairs, the need to promote partnership and goodwill among religions—based on truthful mutual understanding—has been self-evident for a long time. This paved the way for the inter-religious movement and the beginning of dialogues between religions. But now, it is becoming increasingly clear that this timely move—for which Dr Hans Küng, Rev. M.M. Thomas, Bishop Piero Rossano and such eminent people have invested so much of their genius and time—stands in need of renewal and a greater sense of direction.

The interfaith movement has sought to make peace between religions, just as the United Nations has endeavoured to preserve and promote peace between nations. The approaches and the outcome, in both instances, have been similar. Both have done a great deal of good and have gone as far as they could. But they have not gone far enough. An uneasy peace prevails in both sectors. Peace as a positive state of shared commitments to build a better world—free from the evils of deprivation, disabilities, discrimination, exploitation and injustice—continues to elude us. This is not to underplay the significance of what has been achieved in both sectors so far. This is only to argue that the time has come for us to take the next logical step forward.

The inter-religious movement has not come to terms with the full implications of religious exclusivism and the unspiritual dynamics of religion-based community building. Religious communities are formed on the principles of inclusion and exclusion, even when their scriptures militate against this very logic. Religious scriptures, except in patches where they have been tampered with, are perforce inclusive in spirit. But all religious communities are exclusive in practice. They are what people outside of their folds are not. The interfaith dialogue has not grasped this core reality. Instead, it has allowed it to be confined to certain religious pockets without impacting the general outlook of the people. The time has come for the interfaith movement to become a genuine people's movement, rather than its remaining confined in the hands of the religious elite. If it doesn't, it will not attain its full stature as a movement; it will remain an 'ism' or an ideology—'interfaith-ism', if you like.

The root cause of religious exclusivism, which generates an attitude of hostility towards other faiths, is the polarization between the priestly and the prophetic elements in religion. The spiritual health and dynamism of every religious tradition rest on an integration of these two key elements. But as a religious tradition becomes increasingly institutionalized, the priestly class begins to dominate and eventually outlaws the prophetic element in its outlook and culture. The priest, especially when he rejects the prophetic breadth of vision, tends to be a fierce proponent and custodian of the interests of the religious establishment which are indistinguishable from his own class interests. The prophet, in contrast, stands for a universal vision, and especially the spiritual duty to practise justice and righteousness in respect of so-called 'aliens and strangers'. The priest emphasizes the otherness of others. The prophet underlines the kinship of others. Exclusiveness is the priestly dogma; universal oneness is the prophetic creed.

The ideal, of course, is the integration of the prophet and the priest. It was such an ideal that we have in the cherished memory of Bishop Piero Rossano and it is right and proper that we pay glowing tributes to him today. But to do that in a meaningful way is to take the work of this enlightened man of God to its logical and theological conclusion.

The track record of the interfaith movement so far indicates that this integration of the priestly and the prophetic has not yet been achieved. But this is the summit that we need to scale in the days ahead. As long as the priestly agenda dominates the religious establishments of the world, the interfaith movement will remain only peripheral and occasional stirring; 'beating in the void', as an English poet said in a different context, its 'luminous wings in vain'.

SOCIAL TRANSFORMATION

Barring glorious exceptions in history, religion has mostly played a role in maintaining the status quo, rather than a transformative role. This is due to the erroneous idea of religion itself, which now needs to be radically reviewed. The key issues here are:

(i) **The idea of God:** As long as God is projected in a territorial, partisan or racist manner, the logic for religions to move from conflict to cooperation will not become intelligible to people. The idea of God, preached and popularized in every religious constituency, is virtually contrary to the idea of God illumined by its own scripture. The Bible says, for instance, that God does not practise partiality. But Christians are made to believe that their God is partial to them, and that He has a malicious delight in consigning non-Christians to hell. In the Vedic tradition, God is without any physical attribute, yet countless idols are made to mock the Formless One in all sorts of forms, both beautiful and grotesque. Unless we have the courage and intellectual integrity to encounter God as God—and not as some doctrinal or sectarian idol of our own making—we shall not move from 'interfaith-ism' to 'interfaith movement' or universal kinship.

(ii) **The idea of the human family:** It is a spiritual insight shared by all religious traditions that the Creator God is equally the source of all life. In

Christian thought, the myth of Adam and Eve is meant to emphasize the oneness of the whole species. This is also true of other faiths. Yet religion has been the foremost instrument for social stratification and fragmentation. Religion has been invoked, one way or another, to legitimize race and caste. This has been done by effecting a polarization between faith and reason, thereby robbing the people of their right and duty to think for themselves—to seek truth and to practise justice. The greatest atrocity that religions inflict upon humankind is propagating 'blind faith': foisting unreflective conformity to absurd ideas and practices as a sacred duty—ideas and practices which would otherwise be rejected out of hand. By unfurling a myriad of taboos and irrational fears—for example, hell or uncomplimentary rebirths after death—the merchants of religion have enforced irrational conformity on their unwitting and credulous co-religionists, especially in respect of those core spiritual insights in every religious tradition that together comprise the shared spiritual heritage of our species.

The quintessential business of religion is to reinforce a sense of universal kinship. Instead, religion has been misused and abused as an excuse for erecting walls of division and separation.

Religious nurture, as it has been in vogue, has made people obsessed with superficial differences and blind to the deep, underlying unity. As a result, people have been stripped of their ability to cope with differences creatively, which is the basic spiritual discipline all genuine religious cultures must foster. Owing to this, even the inter-religious initiative has become sidetracked by focusing only on superficial similarities. Thus, it unwittingly created the impression that 'differences' are anathema—which was also what the fundamentalists were saying. While the fundamentalists tried to attack and eliminate differences, the dialogists glossed over differences and pretended that they did not exist, or that they did not matter, even if they did. This foreclosed the prospect of a full and genuine or truthful inter-religious dialogue.

What we need is not a uniform and regimented world, but a united world: a global community that is spiritually strong enough to admit and transcend differences and turn them into means of enrichment, rather than items of offence and mutual alienation. Unless we insist, in theory and practice, that all people—black and white, rich and poor—have the same worth in the eyes of God, the interfaith movement will not become the force that it can be.

(iii) **The idea of reality:** The escapist model of religion cannot accept the logic of integration that the inter-religious movement calls for. The main motivation for forging interfaith partnerships is to address the burning issues of our world. As long as people are taught either that these realities do not matter, or that they will be recompensed in the world to come, the scope for spiritual dynamism does not even come into view. Fatalism and hypothetically proffered substitute gratifications are both priestly inventions to domesticate the people and to forestall the revolutionary urge in them. Religion must be a quest for perfection here upon this earth, and not just the offer of a 'pie-in-the-sky-when-you-die'. The time has come for the religions of the world to unite in addressing the escalating problems of the global community. Only in this dynamic partnership will we understand each other in truth and discover the resources of our solidarity. Only this will catalyse the spirituality of each religious tradition, without which we cannot talk meaningfully of our *shared spirituality*.

(iv) **The place of scripture:** There is, on the one hand, the need to return to the authentic scripture, both in terms of the text and its interpretation. And on the other, there is a need to critique the idolatry of scripture. All scriptures are mixed-up affairs. There is much in them of undying and eternal value. But there is also a great deal that needs to be subjected to rational and historical scrutiny. Scripture needs to be tested on the touchstone of life. The primacy of life demands that whatever is anti-life and socially iniquitous, even if it may claim scriptural warrant, needs to be discarded. Scripture and traditions that warrant a relationship of conflict with other religions or ethnic groups belong to this category. Anything that even remotely justifies inequality, injustice and the domination of one man by another is incompatible with the spirituality of life. It should have no place in any scripture that claims to be sacred or revealed; for it is an affront to God, from whom the specific inhuman prescription is purported to have been received.

(v) **The role of culture:** The interfaith movement needs to come to terms with the question of culture. Especially in this age of scientific secularism, people live and act in terms of the presuppositions and priorities of their culture, rather than of their religion. In the past, the encounters between religions were essentially encounters between cultures. For example, it was the arbitrarily claimed superiority of Western culture that became the mainstay for the notion of Christianity's superiority over other religions. Contrary to its decidedly Eastern origins, Christianity has been equated with Western culture. In India, we are also battling obscurantist forces that equate upper-caste culture with Hinduism.

Wherever religion is uncritically equated with a culture, it acquires fundamentalist and imperialist tendencies. Both Islam and Christianity have suffered grievously on account of this equation. Rather than identify itself with a culture, the spiritual task is to be vigilant against the aberrations and injustices that all cultures abound in. Perhaps it is necessary for us now to contemplate the possibility that the interfaith movement was also envisaged within a cultural perspective that needs to be critiqued spiritually.

(vi) **The offence of social transformation:** Transformation is not just any change. It is even more than a change for the better. It is a radical change that empowers the fulfilment of potentialities that remain hidden and untapped. The scope of transformation goes beyond that of reform. Reform is content with specific improvements, whereas transformation calls for shifting the very foundation on which a society or religious system is based. It is a total and comprehensive agenda.

We need to acknowledge that reform movements have, by and large, fared poorly in the religious context. Either they have been snuffed out, or their proponents have been cast out by the religious elite. In the latter instance, reform movements themselves became religious sects or denominations. It is unrealistic, hence, to talk of interfaith initiatives for social transformation, without due recognition of the challenges and roadblocks which are to be encountered.

The prospect of any radical change will make the managers of the existing scheme of things aggressively defensive. Since religion itself has a track record of reinforcing the status quo, it is unlikely that the mere coming together of religions, without their own spiritual transformation, can begin to address the stiff challenge of social transformation. As a rule, only that which is transformed can be an instrument of transformation. The spiritual deepening and inward liberation of all religions is integral to this process. However, it is unrealistic to insist that the spiritual transformation of religions is a precondition for this process to begin. Instead, this should be a clear and primary goal of the interfaith movement.

(vii) **Interfaith initiatives in the Indian context:** The peculiar needs and opportunities of the Indian context inspired some of us to launch, some years ago, a major multi-religious initiative. Most of us had the background of interfaith dialogue; and we also shared a certain degree of disenchantment with it. Experience had convinced us that unless we moved from the *dialogue of words* to the *dialogue of deeds* we could not address the needs of the times. It was also clear to us that the focus on social justice had to be the necessary thrust. The result was the formation of Religions for Social Justice, in order to unite religions in the pursuit of social justice in the Indian context.

The earliest public programme undertaken under the auspices of Religions for Social Justice was a multi-religious pilgrimage to Manoharpur, where the Australian missionary Graham Staines and his two sons had been burned alive by Hindu fanatics. This was the first pilgrimage of its kind; it turned out to be a powerful and transformative experience for all those who participated in it. In the process of seeking together truth and justice, all of us were able to get past the divisive, superficial labels of religions, and experience a deep spiritual oneness. Since then, the united voice of religions—under the auspices of this multi-religious movement—has been heard in respect of several key issues that face our society, whether it be fighting the evils of drug and alcohol abuse, dowry deaths, gender injustice, caste oppression or deaths due to hunger as well as poverty.

One significant initiative has been to maintain an interfaith presence in the national media. For the first time in the history of Indian journalism, articles co-authored by people of different religions have been published regularly in national dailies. This, along with other such initiatives, is aimed at creating and projecting multi-religious partnerships at a time when religious fanatics are trying hard to thicken the walls of religious divide and aggravate alienation between faiths.

While we are happy that some breakthroughs are indeed happening, we are also concerned that centuries of negative religious conditioning continue to keep the common man a slave to irrational fears and mutual suspicion, even in the face of closer interfaith cooperation. The religious establishment itself speaks in different tones on this issue: in theory it endorses the inter-religious model, but in practice it contradicts or discourages it. The excessive anxiety excited by the prospect of practical cooperation between religions in the service of common causes is a symptom of the unhealthy religious conditioning that continues to hold sway. This is mainly the hangover of the competitive model of relationships; it continues to breed deep-seated, mutual distrust among religious communities.

The situation will improve, though, once we move gradually from the erstwhile model of growing at each other's expense to sharing a common mission. The trend so far has been to try to sort out theological differences so as to pave the way for partnerships. This is to put the cart before the horse. Theological riddles will be resolved automatically when we come closer together and share a mission. We need to experience each other, through what we share and struggle for, if at all we are to know each other. Knowledge, except of the shallow and theoretical kind, comes only in the wake of experience. Spirituality is a domain of depth experience. Superficial knowledge lends itself to manipulation, whereas in-depth knowledge dismantles walls of alienation and promotes a sense of kinship or oneness.

The goal of social transformation is important and attainable, provided a genuine and spiritually dynamic interfaith movement is initiated. The extent to which this may become a reality will depend largely on our willingness to accept the changes and corrections that this calls for. As Jesus of Nazareth said: 'New wine cannot be put into old wineskins.' The emerging global scenario offers an unprecedented opportunity to evolve a spirituality conducive to creative interfaith initiatives. Today, interfaith movement is not a theological luxury; it is a practical and historic necessity. Standing in the twilight of the new order, we are all the more impressed and grateful for the pioneering work of men and women of vision in this sphere. They have earned our eternal gratitude by serving as signposts to point us to the destination that awaits us. Insofar as we continue to ascend the steps of spiritual exploration and practical initiatives, and take their work a step nearer towards perfection, we express our gratitude to them in ways that mere words can never hope to encapsulate.

3

Religions for Social Justice

Global developments in the last two decades have precipitated a number of existential and spiritual questions that need to be addressed squarely. All of us—the six billion human beings that comprise the global community—are profoundly affected by these developments. The emerging world order has thrown up challenging issues with sharp edges, particularly for those of us in non-Western societies.

Words like globalization, privatization, liberalization, structural adjustment, market economy and so on have lost their newness. We get the smell of global order in our neighbourhood. Its colours and sounds pour into our living rooms via satellites. The very feel of our environment has changed. Our sense of independence is becoming dimmer day by day. We feel as if we are thrown into an unfamiliar, inhospitable economic and cultural orbit that fills our intuitions with anxiety. This loss of control is deeply unnerving.

We in the East are not smart change managers. We have an uncanny knack for turning the means for empowerment into instruments of disability. That is what we have done with our religions. God was too generous to us in this respect. Religions have been our main items of produce and export. They have done well as exiles and explorers elsewhere; Buddhism is a case in point. At home we have degraded religion into obscurantism and escapism. Also, most lamentably, we have used religion as an instrument for oppression and exploitation; this is clearly the case with the caste system, the most ingenious device ever invented by man to perpetuate the oppressive status quo.

Three limitations have forestalled the unique situation in India from eventuating into a spiritual revolution. The first is the ascendancy of a ritualistic and formulaic approach to religion. People have fostered a shallow religiosity that saw religion in isolation from their day-to-day life and the aches and pains of the world around them. Life, however, has been lived according to the demands of the world: its politics, economics, culture and so on. Periodically, one has returned to religion for repair work so that one's pursuits did not suffer.

Second, religions themselves have functioned in separate and mutually exclusive spheres, at a safe distance from each other. While their relationships have not been characterized by overwhelming hostility, there has been no active cooperation between them either. Spatially and socially they have shared little in common. As a matter of fact, attempts have been made to preserve the dividing walls between religions, as this has been beneficial to the dominant powers at all times. This has called for a focus on the surface (where differences abound), to the total exclusion of the inner core where the spirit of oneness resides.

Third, the secular rhetoric has further legitimized the dichotomy between religion and social public life by insisting on the privatization of religion. Religion has been tolerated only in the private domain, and considered an unwelcome trespasser into the public space. With this advocacy, secularism has seen only spectres of religion, and been blind to the treasures of true spirituality. It has envisaged social engineering and nation building as value-neutral enterprises, wherein only material resources are relevant.

Practical experience as well as the witness of

history proves convincingly that these outlooks have been an invitation to disaster. Our doctrines and world view robbed us of our historic dynamism; we became inward-looking. Soon we succumbed to forces from beyond our borders, with which we had no means of coping. A millennium of enslavement followed, which ended in 1947—or so we were made to believe.

But in independent India, millions continue to be strangers to freedom. They languish in the prisons of poverty, illiteracy and caste oppression. The reconstruction of India since attaining independence more than six decades ago has faltered for want of an adequate spiritual culture. Oppression of the powerless continues unabated. Social, religious and economic justice is not available to Dalits and those of the lower castes. The poor and lower-caste people continue to be socially degraded and alienated from the fruits of development. Our society is becoming more and more violent. National priorities do not reflect human needs and social realities. Our society has disintegrated due to corruption. Religion, which is meant to lead people to freedom and dignity, has been progressively alienated from our public life in the name of secularism.

The apathy of those in authority towards human need and avoidable suffering continues; the voice of the powerless is becoming feebler and feebler. The invisibility of the poor has reached unprecedented proportions in the wake of globalization. The floodgates have been opened for multinational corporation (MNC) predators. Our external debt has soared: it stands at US $440.6 billion, an astronomical figure that could break the back of future generations. This has cost us our independence. And it is a concern of particular consequence for the illiterate masses, who are largely unaware that each of them is born with a burden of debt.

The elite have abandoned the poor to their slavery. One out of every three Indians is languishing in a condition of servitude; the rich have hoarded the fruits of freedom for themselves. Religions have failed human beings in their struggle for meaning and dignity, for justice and equity. They have inflicted non-healing wounds on our national psyche due to their adversarial attitude to each other. And they have discredited themselves by their culpable blindness to social realities.

It is painful for any patriotic person to take this uncomplimentary view of the Indian scenario. Clearly, religions need to foster a modern and scientific outlook, which would mean that they have to discard many of the unscientific and irrational beliefs that form the basis of most of their dogma.

The common man no longer turns to religion for inspiration to become a better human being. People expect no public good to come from religion. Escapist religiosity now thrives more robustly than ever before. In the era of liberalization, temples, gurudwaras, mosques and churches have become richer, more crowded and busier. Places of worship have become a haven for parking ill-gotten wealth, amassed by those who are in the race for making quick money. Credibility of religious leaders is at its lowest ebb. What is most intriguing is that they stand in isolation from the burning issues of our times. Even the West, which was willing to be mesmerized by our god-men, is already disillusioned and sceptical. One can understand their perspective. There are simply too many fake swamis around.

A century ago, Swami Vivekananda spoke euphorically about the spiritual destiny of India that needed to be fulfilled in the global arena, to the benefit of the entire human species. That dream has not been fulfilled. Let us admit that our dreams and our deeds went their separate ways, creating a national crisis that threatens to turn our dreams into nightmares. Today it is a global nightmare; a nightmare of human crisis, of mounting poverty in the midst of multiplying wealth, and of escalating inequality in a world that resounds with the egalitarian rhetoric of unimaginable social injustice. Man's cruelty to man has been aggravated, rather than ameliorated, by the freedom of a few and the enslavement of the rest.

The voice of Vivekananda reverberated in the citadel of materialism, in an eloquent call to rediscover the lost spiritual vision of the human species. He saw this as primarily the fulfilment of the spiritual genius of India, and then the evolution of the human species as a whole. Much has changed since then. The precarious balance between materialism and spiritual culture has only tilted further in favour of materialism, paving the way for a steep fall in the values underlying human life. The instruments of international control have gained unimaginable powers of coercion. The capacity of the poorer nations to resist the cultural onslaught to which they are subject has declined further. And the juggernaut of economics and trade has broken loose from the controls of democracy and compulsions of politics.

Anxiety is mounting all over the world, and like the biblical Tower of Babel, the gigantic structures we have created could come crashing down and crush our future. In less than two decades, our honeymoon with globalization has begun to sour, paving the way for the realization that unless the global order is fortified by an appropriate and adequate spiritual vision, it could turn into a gas chamber for our humanity. 'Man,' as Jesus forewarned two millennia ago, 'does not live by bread alone.' This is a truth that continues to stare at us even today. The materialistic misconception to the contrary—offering bread at the cost of our humanity—can only end in robbing the poor of the crumbs on which they survive.

To create a world order, and not enunciate an appropriate spiritual vision for the global community, is positively suicidal. People the world over have begun to feel the tremor it has created. To throw the nations and peoples of the world together in an economic pell-mell, without addressing the divisiveness and bankruptcy of religions—as they have been re-crafted in this century and practised—is an act of irresponsibility. Why is this so?

To ask this question is also to ask what we mean by religion. Reduced to its essentials, the religions of the world address essentially the question, as Tolstoy pointed out so aptly, of our vertical and horizontal relationships. In spiritual terms, this is the need that all human beings have to know and love God and to love one another. The joys and sorrows of our life are born out of our relatedness. The closer we get to people and groups, the greater is the problem of their otherness. Proximity is a unique human paradox, given the fact that we are meant to be social beings. We need to belong. To belong is to come closer. But to come closer is to intensify the problems of differences. At a distance, differences do not offend. They hurt in nearness. This is human nature.

Different religious communities have coexisted over the millennia in the Indian subcontinent, in greater peace and harmony than in any other part of the world. But of late, the tensions between some communities have intensified. This is largely due to the closer proximity between religious communities brought about by the age of communication and increased mobility. Knowledge is a category of nearness. You are not far away from what you know. Now, the custodians of various religions know a great deal more about each other than they did ever before.

This increased knowledge about each other need not necessarily aggravate the hostility of religious communities. What makes this otherwise desirable development a source of trouble is the fact that religions have seated themselves in conflict zones. They look at each other in terms of differences and are blind to what they share in common. The call of the times is centripetal; it pulls religions together. But religions, in their attitude to each other, are centrifugal; they pull away from each other. This state of affairs is more dynamic than that which prevailed until recently, where religions were confined to their separate constituencies. It is ironic and significant that the growing nearness of religions has resulted in heightened tensions among them.

Globalization will necessarily blur the familiar national boundaries. The distances between and among nations will diminish. Continents will come closer. Cultures will bump into each other. Languages will cross-fertilize to a greater extent than they did in the age of colonialism. World views will struggle for survival space. An unprecedented level of human desperation could result in many parts of the world, especially in non-Western societies. The human predicament will come under further pressure.

In such a scenario, religions can no longer afford to play their customary adversarial roles and compete among themselves in order to maximize their respective advantages or thrive at each other's expense. Nor can they hope to prolong an uneasy truce, by limiting their spheres of operation in the interest of communal harmony—which is a negative strategy. Harmony, if understood only as an absence of tension because of ghettoizing, is hardly of spiritual value. Harmony of the dynamic kind calls for an active interaction among the religions of the world, and the formation of a shared forum for addressing the pressing issues of the global community.

Religions are meant to help people cope with life. They are a call to transform individuals and societies. Religion is, or is meant to be, the foremost ally of the human species in its quest for dignity, meaning and fulfilment in life. That being so, religions contradict themselves when they retreat from the life of the people to their own lives as institutions. Religion is a call to engagement, rather than escapism.

Historically, religions have emerged from the furnace of human life. The engagement with suffering, and not worldly indulgence, has been the stimulant for the spiritual evolution of our species. But suffering will not result in spiritual deepening if religion is allowed to be escapist.

Even as materialism mounts, and the agonies of social and personal life intensify, people are ever more turning to ritualistic and escapist versions of religions. Religiosity has increased rather than decreased in recent times. This religiosity serves as an adjunct to the prevailing system, and not as a resource for transforming peoples and societies.

Indeed, there is no dearth of religiosity in India, or elsewhere in the world. On the contrary, we are suffering from a surfeit of religiosity, especially of the cultic kind. Gurus multiply by the hour, and the shadows of guru-dom lengthen over humankind. Religions threaten to become liabilities. Though they are meant to be a unifying force, religions have of late become sources of division and alienation to an extent rarely seen before. Instead of nurturing and ennobling our humanity, communal passions unleashed by religions inhibit and corrupt our native goodness. Hate, rather than love, is being preached and practised. Injustice, when it is sanctioned by religion, is more difficult to combat and contain. This is a serious threat to the health and integrity of our lives.

The need of the hour is to shift from religiosity to spirituality. Rituals, dogmas and communal interests belong to the surface of religions; all the more so in a commercial and consumerist context, where religion is driven by covetousness. Spirituality comprises the deeper core of religions. Justice is the essence of spirituality. In a legal sense, justice is mostly a matter of redressing individual and, at times, collective grievances. Spiritually, justice calls for the creation of wholesome conditions for life and the affirmation of basic values, whereby human beings are helped to attain fullness and find fulfilment in life. Spiritually, justice has a social foundation; for we are social beings.

Vis-à-vis the global scenario, today we stand at a crossroads. From here, we can take either of two following paths. With the first, by default we can be a party to the tragedy of non-Western cultures and religions being superseded by Western culture and its acquired religious arm of Christianity. This prospect seems to have influenced Pope John Paul II's vision for the Church in Asia, as enunciated in the synodal document released in Delhi recently. It reflects not so much the spirit of biblical Christianity as the hegemonic and invasive spirit of Western culture, which equates its ideas with the fate of the global community!

Consequently, globalization would, in reality, amount to nothing more than westernization and Christianization—which is different from evangelization. Evangel is 'good news', and the good news shared by all religions is that we are all equally the children of God, and have an eternal destiny. It is also that in true spirituality, we have all the resources we need to transform individuals and societies alike. Religion, when it is understood and practised according to scriptural ideals, is potentially a mighty weapon to defeat the forces of oppression and exploitation, to usher in a new heaven and new earth.

Surprisingly, Christians seldom wonder why the biblical vision deems it necessary to long for a 'new heaven', and not merely for 'a new earth'. Is it not because they too, like others, have corrupted both heaven and earth and remade their God after their own image, to suit their vested interests from time to time? If God is indeed the same as many of them have understood and preached for these many centuries, it cannot but create an identity crisis for heaven as the seat of the Christian God. It makes heaven not such an exciting place, after all!

The second of the two roads could take us in an entirely new direction. It would call for a new paradigm of interfaith relations and perceptions. Religions would be relocated in a climate of mutual stimulation and shared commitment to human well-being. They would deepen their respective spiritual roots, not to be one up on their neighbours, but to bring their wealth into the comity of religions for the further ennoblement of the human species. The worth of religions will no longer be measured in terms of the size of their religious communities, which is necessary to negate the spirit of competition among them. As with religions, so with cultures. The spirit of hegemony will be mastered by a sense of shared destiny and our collective stewardship of the human species.

It is a nightmarish prospect for the poor and powerless societies of the world to be incorporated into a world order uninformed by spiritual values and moral imperatives. In the absence of the moral demand, it is crass power that dictates human affairs. Justice and equity fail to keep poverty in check in systems shaped by power. It is the role of spirituality, therefore, to bridle power with a sense of fellow humanity, so that all the bones are not monopolized by the strongest of dogs. It is the business of spirituality to make us better than dogs, in sharing earth's resources. But for this to happen at all, it is imperative that the global community is helped to internalize the appropriate spiritual values.

These values—which are found in various faiths—are not the exclusive property of any one religion. Religions are like pearl beads; they are to be strung together to form a chain of beauty. But that is not the way religions have been viewed so far. The stockists and retailers of religion have been too preoccupied with protecting their own religious wares to develop the spiritual resources to empower and enrich human life. But this cannot go on. Every religion will be called upon, in the days ahead, to account for itself in terms of its transformative and empowering engagement with the human situation—particularly with the plight of the poor and the oppressed.

Religions cannot any longer afford to perpetuate the fatal foolishness of seeing each other as enemies, and in the process lose sight of their real adversaries. The enemies of a religion cannot be other religions. The enemies of a religion are poverty, injustice, illiteracy, exploitation, discrimination, and all that subverts the spiritual goal of fullness of life for all people.

A good Samaritan, anywhere in the world, is haunted by a very basic question: is God responsible for the birth of millions of our children into extremely poor circumstances, leaving about 40,000 of our children to die every day of hunger? And that too in the midst of plenty and opulence? The answer one gets from Vedas, Vedic literature and great Vedic scholars and reformers like Swami Dayanand as also Karl Marx is that God or the Creator of the universe is certainly not responsible for the suffering of the poor. It is the social, economic and political systems we human beings create that are responsible for this cruelty to mankind. Poverty is wholly man-made and it can be eradicated by man. We who believe in a compassionate and just God have a duty to fight this exploitative and unjust social and economic order and bring, as Jesus of Nazareth said, the Kingdom of God on Earth.

What is this Kingdom of God? The sun, moon, stars, air, water, earth, mineral wealth and electronic air waves, etc., are creations of God; they are without discrimination for all people and are for all living creatures. No one has the right to appropriate these natural resources, to profit at the expense of the billions of children of God.

Some of us in India are involved in a new initiative: an exciting socio-spiritual enterprise to prepare the way for a paradigm shift. Leaders from various religious traditions—Hinduism, Islam, Christianity, Sikhism, Buddhism, Jainism and the Baha'i faith—have come together to constitute a multi-faith forum; a 'voice crying in the wilderness' against social oppression and communal aggression. We have discovered the liberating truth that true spirituality is not the exclusive preserve of any particular religious tradition, but the common heritage of the human species. We are also convinced that spirituality is a call to practise justice and to liberate the oppressed. It is also a call to exercise vigilance over the moral and social health of our societies. In the few years that Religions for Social Justice has been in existence in India, several of its multi-religious initiatives have elicited widespread popular and media interest. The three basic goals of this movement are:

i. To relocate religions in a paradigm of mutual cooperation and of dialogue for active engagement with social and political realities.
ii. To project social justice as the essence of true spirituality and to rescue religions from their escapist and obscurantist moulds, to which they have been consigned for centuries.
iii. To evolve a new and appropriate spiritual outlook conducive to social and political cohesion, so that religion becomes a resource for nation building, rather than a communal stumbling block.

The concern for the well-being of those who do not have the means and might to fight for their rights is essentially a spiritual one. In its spiritual core, every religion exhorts us to be kind and generous to the needy, compassionate to those who suffer and to stand by the oppressed; for we all belong together and are equally the children of God. We comprise a cosmic family and a family is only as rich as its poorest member. The hallmark of a family is that none of its members is dispensable or unimportant. Family, to the extent that it is an institution of love, remains free from the dominance of vested interests.

Contrastingly, institutions and systems get dominated by individual and group interests that seek to tilt the balance of convenience in their favour. Privilege, not justice, marks organized life. Unless continued spiritual vigilance is exercised, therefore, injustice and oppression could overrun a society over a period of time—as has been the case with our society. Gandhi's self-identification with the poor and the untouchables was an expression of his spirituality. Independent India has succumbed to corruption concomitantly with, and proportionate to, the abandonment of her religious vision.

The need of the hour is not a divorce between religion and politics, as is advocated by secularists. The need is, on the contrary, to make the state and the society alike conform to universal spiritual norms and values. While religions must be judged in terms of their current practices, they must also be evaluated in terms of a core spiritual vision. Highlighting the contradiction between the two is the prophetic task of our times. It unveils the need to reform and renew religions and regenerate the spiritual foundations of our society. It is this purpose that underlines the founding of Religions for Social Justice.

Today, religion is politicized and politics is communalized. In this process, the people in need are lost sight of. The ascendancy of vested interests threatens to splinter our society and cripple our country. Avoidable suffering and deprivation mount. The foremost need of the hour is a spiritual regeneration so as to imbue progress with social justice and moral passion. Religions for Social Justice is envisaged as a people's movement, to attain this end.

The very first programme undertaken under the auspices of Religions for Social Justice—as mentioned earlier—was a multi-religious pilgrimage to Manoharpur, where the Australian missionary and social worker Graham Staines and his two children were burned alive in the night of 22–23 January 1999. In the wake of this terrible event—which wounded the very soul of India—a group of fifty-one religious leaders, representing the major religious traditions of India, visited Baripada and Manoharpur. It sent the message loud and clear that, irrespective of religious differences, none who are spiritually sensitive can condone such atrocities, and further, that all must be free to acknowledge the glow of the spirit wherever it is found. Spirituality must, and does, rise above communal loyalties. In the large-heartedness and spiritual generosity of Gladys Staines, who spontaneously forgave the killers of her husband and children, we find a reflection of the divine, no matter what religion we follow. This message was articulated throughout the country, through press conferences and several articles that were published after the pilgrimage; it had a powerful national impact.

Religions for Social Justice aims to create an active forum for uniting the various religious traditions that flourish in this country. Their scattered existence—insulated both from the burning issues of the times and from each other—is the root cause for their ineffectiveness in creating a society based on the foundations of justice and peace. Given the needs and challenges of today, the dialogue between religions cannot be limited to words and concepts. Religions must discover a shared agenda, to promote the good of all people and to safeguard the health of the society. This will effect a paradigm shift—from conflict to cooperation, from communalism to spiritual humanism—through which religions will become a constructive, rather than destructive, influence on societies and nations.

As they developed throughout history—and especially since the Renaissance—religions became identified with cultures and nation states. This is out of sync with the logic of a globalizing world.

Ironically, the seeds of globalization lie buried deep in spirituality, which is the only authentically universal vision that humankind has ever had. It is doubtful that any international organization would have come into being, but for the pattern that existed already in spirituality. Unlike the mechanisms of institutionalized religions, the call of true spirituality has always been to transcend the familiar boundaries drawn by individual and corporate ego, and to discover the unity underlying the diversity which marks our world.

As a matter of fact, the very purpose of human spiritual formation is to train people in the art of coping with differences constructively, and to turn variety into an opportunity for enrichment rather than a liability. Thus, while religion may see the non-itself as its adversary, from a spiritual perspective, even the enemy is part of the larger body of the human species, and so cannot be excised or excluded. This is the secret of health and wholeness for a society. It is out of this inalienable belonging that the compulsions of justice and compassion are born. Injustice, on the other hand, thrives by distorting otherness into hostility or a source of pollution. It is for this reason that tribes, castes and groups that have been subjected to systemic oppression have always been caricatured as subhuman or as sources of pollution. The precept of pollution is that of dehumanization; it is a religiously sanctioned rejection of the humanity of the victim. In such a context, true spirituality cannot but assume a subversive role, the reason being, as Jesus of Nazareth said, that no prophet is accepted among his own people.

In the days ahead, we may not have any use for a spirituality that leaves the oppressors untroubled. And peace should not be allowed to degenerate into the rhetoric of the establishment. The spirituality for the emerging global order cannot afford to be a compendium of nice and toothless sentiments. The oppressed and miserable people of the world have no use for such pious ornaments. They are not looking for improved cages—they are crying out for freedom. They long to be airborne and belong to the heavens. The heart of our global spirituality must, therefore, be an uncompromising commitment to social justice. The cultures of the world must be graded no longer, as the West used to do, on the scale of their rationality, but on the basis of their commitment to social justice. A society that is unmindful of the claims of social justice must be branded primitive.

And the global community must evolve effective instruments to enforce agreed norms of justice on the systems and governments of the world. The argument that social justice is an 'internal affair' of nation states should no longer be entertained. In a globalizing world, fundamental values and bottom line justice should not be left to the charity of nation states. But we do not have, as of now, an instrument with sufficient credibility and moral authority—free from the angularities of a global order based on power and inequality—to address this task.

Spirituality is not an anthology of multi-faith dogmas or scriptures. Instead, it is the priorities and compulsions that emerge through an active engagement with the given context, from a position of love for humankind and reverence towards God. Spirituality is the foremost resource for human empowerment. But empowerment itself can be—and, indeed, has mostly been—understood culturally, rather than spiritually. The common understanding of empowerment in the West, which has been adopted by the rest of the global community, amounts mostly to negotiations of power sharing. To empower is to equip a deprived individual or group to negotiate effectively with the systems and powers that be, so as to share the resources and opportunities in the given context. While this is important in the scheme of things, this is not the final reach of empowerment in the spiritual paradigm. The goal of empowerment is not only to negotiate power sharing, but also to transcend the power paradigm itself in the macro situation. The more that spiritual principles and patterns are resented, the greater is the need for spiritual initiatives and interventions.

Every human being needs to be empowered to attain the fullness of his/her hidden human scope. And conditions conducive to the full unfolding of the human potential in all people must be created. History bears witness to the fact that such a goal cannot be achieved within the current paradigm of power. The business of true spirituality, in the end, is for love to supersede power as the shaping paradigm for the human species. The essence of the spiritual light that all great religious seers have brought is the need for the human species to shift from the love of power to the power of love. Compassion, fellow feeling, selfless commitment to an altruistic cause, the spirit of sacrificial service, social justice, and respect for human worth and human equality are all authentic expressions of the power of love—whereas the love of power sees them either as superfluous or as liabilities.

If the emerging global order is not imbued with the imperatives of such a spiritual paradigm shift, there can be no guarantee that it will be different in spirit and scope from the old colonial exploitation. This nightmare looms large over the horizon of 'the children of the lesser gods', who account for two-thirds of the world's population. We must address this issue in a serious and sustained way over the coming years.

Gandhi taught us that greed in general—and the greed for power in particular—is the source of all evil. He therefore put forth a remarkable and rational view on the question of power, its nature and the need for restricting it to the bare minimum. In his scheme of things, as society becomes more and more enlightened, the state and its powers should be proportionately decentralized and minimized at all levels. Karl Marx arrived at an almost identical conclusion. But the big difference in the two lay in the means they advocated. While means were not important to the disciples of Karl Marx, they were paramount to Gandhi. Gandhi's means were determined by the eternal truths. Therefore, he used love and compassion as weapons against the world's greatest imperial power.

Gandhi once told a journalist that what he found most remarkable about people in positions of power was how hard of heart they were. He therefore prescribed to his 'disciples', who were soon to assume political power in India, that whatever policies they adopted should be aimed at removing tears from the last man's eyes in the lowest rung of society. Only then, he said, would the power of government benefit everyone. Gandhi gave a talisman to the first prime minister of India, and through him to all successive prime ministers and the ruling elite. This, in his own words, was: 'Whenever you are in doubt, recall the face of the poorest and the most hapless man you have ever seen, and ask yourself if the step you contemplate is going to be of any use to him: will it restore to him a control over his own destiny?' How little his followers heeded this advice is revealed by the budgetary allocations made by the Government of India for human development and social welfare.

Religions of the world must declare a holy war on poverty. We have had two world wars. We need a third one. And that war—the Mother of all Wars—should not stop until the enemy is wiped off the face of this planet. From a spiritual perspective, our foremost enemy is poverty. The poverty of the world is entirely man-made and wholly unnecessary. Nothing discredits the religions of the world more than their disgraceful tolerance of this massive human scandal. The idea of Jesus breaking his body to feed the people has been turned by Christians into some sort of sentimental and mystical mumbo-jumbo. It was nothing of the sort. What Jesus meant by the revolutionary ritual he instituted was the need to develop a culture of sharing, so that everything—not excluding even one's own body—is shared in a sacred commitment to the biblical teaching: 'Do unto others as you would have them do unto you.' The same generosity of spirit is captured by the spiritual glow of other faiths too. This is the spiritual core that needs to be infused into the spirit of the new millennium. We must refuse to sentimentalize or glamorize poverty. Poverty is not a virtue. It is a spiritual scandal; a blot on the face of the Creator.

At the centre of our war on world poverty is the burning question of Third World debt, which today runs into billions of dollars. The most debt-trapped countries are also the poorest in the world. And a sizeable chunk of their meagre annual income is consumed by debt servicing. The anaemic of the world are routinely bled to fatten the rich. A legalistic approach to this life-and-death issue will not do. We need to set the poor societies of the world free from the prison of their debts.

The spirituality for the new millennium must celebrate a renewed global responsibility to protect the integrity of creation. But we must refuse to buy the canard that nature can be saved by some cosmetic changes or technological fine-tuning.

The harsh truth must now be faced. The integrity of creation hinges on our integrity as the carers of creation. The environmental crisis that torments us today is the product of predatory consumerism and unbridled covetousness. Scandalous global inequality and inflated lifestyles—rather than the poor of the world and their multiplication—are what endanger creation. Going by our experience in this field so far, it is obvious that nothing short of a spiritual revolution in the global village can rescue the environment from its present endangered state.

But compassion for creation has to be taken to its full, logical conclusion. How can compassion for creation coexist with cruelty to animals? How can a genuine culture of peace be nurtured, when violence on the non-human world is countenanced? Human beings are meant to be keepers and defenders of life, and not the killers and consumers of life of the animal kingdom.

The equal worth of all human beings, insofar that all embody the divine equally, is the foundation of spirituality. Spirituality is uncompromisingly egalitarian. It denounces every system and ideology, religious or secular, that belittles the worth of human beings. But the last thing that the oppressors want to do is to recognize the humanity or worth of their victims. This is as true of the high priests of the caste system in our country as it was of the architects of apartheid in South Africa. Materialism, in contrast, is perforce an outlook to which inequality of human worth is endemic. The insult inherent with materialism is that it values human beings not for who they are, but for what they have. There can never be any standardization of what human beings may own. Thus, human equality seems an unattainable, even undesirable, goal.

And justice is not egalitarian. Any overt or covert endorsement of inegalitarianism tilts its dispensation in favour of the rich and the powerful, as has happened in all societies. The passion for justice that characterizes all spiritual traditions is based on the equal worth of all human beings. Systemic and endemic injustice has only ever been sustained and legitimized by apportioning unequal worth to different sections of society.

Barring rhetoric, inegalitarianism still remains the operative outlook of the global community. The dangers of this unspiritual outlook could multiply many times on account of globalization. If the worth of human beings is defined in terms of materialistic development, we have to subscribe to an ascending order of human worth calibrated on the scale of material affluence. The life of an American today, for example, is perceived globally as more precious than the life of an African or Asian. Within our own societies, the life of an ordinary citizen is nothing compared to the life of our VVIPs. This is an insult to the spiritual dignity and enlightenment of our species; it is imperative that the global community in the new millennium is freed from this anathema.

Equal opportunities for economic and trade activities—as envisaged in globalization and liberalization—can be a dangerous thing in a world of gross inequalities, where human beings are ascribed unequal worth. Under these conditions, the arrangement that sacrifices billions of lives to prop up the artificial lifestyle of a few million is unlikely to provoke the indignation of the global community. This gives a free hand to the global merchants of death, who wish to sustain regional conflicts in order to secure steady markets for their deadly merchandise. The predatory military–industrial combine, unshackled by moral scruples and unhindered by national or international instruments, is already the ultimate nightmare for the people of two-thirds of the world. Let us not forget that the overwhelming majority of the armed conflicts that have taken place since World War II have been in Asia and Africa. Certainly, the beneficiaries of these accursed death games have not been the miserable wretches from these regions affected by war.

Today we have enough grounds to despair of the possibility that the politics of diplomacy would secure a stable foundation for world peace. All along, diplomacy has preached peace while preparing for war. The cause of world peace will be safe only on spiritual foundations, with an adequate emphasis on the equality of human worth. Poverty has been the foremost catalyst for war. War, in its turn, has also been the foremost cause for the perpetuation of poverty. This vicious cycle is sustained through deliberate human strategies and choices, driven by greed and callousness. The rationale for peace will not dawn on the powers that be, unless the global community as a whole undergoes a spiritual re-education concerning the essentials of peace.

Social justice is the soul of spirituality. In a practical sense, justice and spirituality are synonymous. Both are essentially principles of integration. They are necessary for a society to cohere. An unjust society must undo itself, sooner or later. It is futile and foolish to clamour for social cohesion and national unity, while the divisive and alienating powers of injustice in that society are not contained. The systemic violation of social justice is the primary reason for the endemic disunity in

India. Further, the social legitimization of caste injustice has resulted in the stunting of India's spiritual evolution.

The same is true also in the history of other religions. As and when Christianity became enmeshed with state power and deviated from the paths of justice, it squandered its spiritual substance. Islam too suffered a similar distortion. The rise of materialism has unleashed forces of division and disintegration everywhere. It has aggravated social degradation and communal aggression. The idea of a 'global community' will remain a pipe dream as long as materialism is the sole framework for its formation. It is necessary that we enunciate a spirituality capable of addressing the unprecedented needs of the global order, so that the world situation does not degenerate into a theatre of anarchy and oppression.

Here, the lesson of the disintegration of the erstwhile Soviet Union should not be lost on us. What this historic event proved was not that capitalism is, by comparison, a morally superior ideology or way of life. It is very doubtful if it is. Why, then, has the capitalist system endured and survived? The reason for its greater resilience must be found in something more than merely its capitalism. The socialist bloc was, if anything, more rigorous and exclusive as an empiricaly materialistic enterprise.

The capitalistic societies, in contrast to the Soviet Union, sought to preserve the moral principles and values of their religious tradition. These provided a cohesive influence and nurtured the human sensitivities of their respective societies. Even when they ceased to be explicitly religious societies—as in the case of secular and post-Christian Europe and North America—they continued to operate on the moral foundations that they had acquired through their spiritual formation over the centuries. It will therefore be a fatal mistake to assume that the global community can remain intact and socially wholesome without the integrative influence of true spirituality.

History calls us to venture on to new spiritual terrains and to walk the paths that we have not trodden before. We need to accept this challenge on behalf of our species, to turn the grand experiment of globalization into a life-friendly and just enterprise—and not an eventual monster of inequity and oppression.

God, the supreme giver of life and happiness, is there in every particle and subatomic particle of the universe. He says, 'Oh, my children, enjoy it equally and let no one be greedy to usurp the share of others, because this wealth does not belong to any individual.'

Natural resources are the common property of all people. Therefore, it is certainly *not* God who creates poverty and the poor. It needs to be emphasized: God abhors poverty, because he is the God of Justice. Only Mammon will countenance the creation of inequality and the aggravation of the misery and destitution of masses. The prevailing global order is already under the judgement of God. Its days are numbered. No amount of charity will avert its impending demise. What is needed is repentance: a complete change of heart. The acid test of that repentance will be an all-out effort to eradicate poverty and the threat of terrorism from the face of the earth. This will only happen as a consequence of our regaining the lost spiritual strength of loving our neighbours—that is, neighbouring countries, Afro-Asian countries; indeed, all in the global village—as ourselves.

4

Interfaith Dialogue for Peace

Unquestionably, any discussion on interfaith dialogue should begin with a search for the basic principles of the dialogic method of communication. We must begin to talk with each other; in this age, physical proximity no longer ensures nearness. Proximity without nearness or mutuality could breed cruelty. The thief, no less than the lover, wants to come close. The difference is in what underlies their coming and going. The thief does not abide in his coming: his coming is his going—distant and impersonal. This distance—and an impersonal nature of being with others—has been the logic of violence, especially in colonial history. Violence in this age, which romanticizes and technologizes distance, seems to be a function of proximity. So the global village could degenerate into a crucible of cruelty, if proximity does not deepen into an in-depth encounter leading to oneness. The enlargement of the ambit of mutual understanding is the proof that our proximity is enlivened by an understanding of each other in truth. Proximity vitiated by mistrust cannot but degenerate into violence.

It seems that we live in a world of disrupted communications. For this reason, there is a need to facilitate dialogue: to set up the matrix, mechanisms, means and mindset of dialogue. That is the most important task. The fact that two parties sit face-to-face and engage in exchanges does not necessarily mean that they are dialoguing. Even at the individual level, conversations tend to degenerate into soliloquies interspersed with interrogations. People are in flight from each other, from themselves and from the freedom to love and listen to each other.

The challenge is to sustain the sacrament of dialogue in an age of lovelessness. In the divine plan, communication is the conduit for love. It enables the river of love to flow, deepen and nourish the flower bed of mutual understanding. But when power displaces love, the river of sharing is polluted; it becomes a sewer of alienation that eddies and gurgles only on the surface. So we must begin in the depth, and enunciate a culture of dialogue.

We know that the foundation of a dialogic

culture is love. Love revels in listening no less than in speaking. Love is eagerly reciprocal. When love evaporates, the reciprocity of communication gets deformed into unilateralism: the will to be heard vitiates the willingness to listen. Conversation may also give way to imposition. Violence overwhelms silence. Silence is the essence of dialogue—for it is in silence that we open the sanctuary of the self to the other, where alone the other may be understood in spirit and in truth. A dialogue that does not seek to know the 'other' in a state of hospitality—of unconditional acceptance—rarely goes beyond the cacophony of the surface. The surface is a sphere of diversity without the invisible threads of unity. Life is a dialogue—a ceaseless and ever-deepening flow between the surface and depth. It is this our conversations must seek to imitate.

Listening is rooted in humility. The culture of power mistakes this for weakness. Dialogues can be, and are, undertaken within a paradigm of power. You can see it for what it is. Such dialogues are marked by defensiveness, each walking the landscape of sharing as though it is a minefield of mistrust. This too has its rewards; but they are the elusive trophies of victories and conquests. Communication becomes a denial of communion.

We must be realistic. Dialogue is not a magic

wand with which one can wipe away the nuclear stockpile. The goal of dialogue is to effect a metanoia, a change of mind from within. We cannot stop short of fostering a mental culture that abhors the use of force in all its forms. Force is perforce unilateral. Dialogue is a celebration of mutuality and interdependence. Weapons of mass destruction are symbolic in nature; they, and the psychology that begets them, encapsulate the ruthless exercise of the will to power. The will to power abolishes the space for dialogue. Power is the reigning paradigm of our world. Institutionalized religion itself is predicated on power and its corollary of domination and violence. Those who dialogue cannot afford to overlook this harsh reality.

The primary goal of global dialogue is to create a counterculture. It is to foster a shared faith in the way of peace that refuses to demonize those we dislike or disagree with. It is a commitment to the pilgrim path that engages the *different other* with love, until the hidden treasures of our shared humanity, in its myriad expressions, begin to cohere in the grammar of the spirit. Our task is not to attack weapons of mass destruction; it is not even to despise those who starve millions to amass stockpiles of such weapons. Our task is to interrogate the demonic myth of enmity and to do so constructively, by transforming proximity into the nearness of hearts and minds. Peace is the understanding of the other in love, whereas war caricatures the other in hate. Weapons are merely the idioms of its eloquence. As long as these distortions persist, our agenda will remain unfulfilled—even if we succeed in eliminating the nuclear stockpiles of the world.

The truth is that conventional weapons, including knives, kill more people than so-called weapons of mass destruction. This is not to argue that weapons of mass destruction should be left untouched. No, they must be eliminated from the face of the earth, for they bear witness to the barbarity that lurks beneath our skin-deep civilization. The universal killer is not a weapon—it is the spirit of hate. It is the murderousness bred by covetousness: the murder of compassion. It is this hard reality that we need to countenance in our dialogues. And our dialogue needs to be both between ourselves and with the world beyond the venues of our conferences. The ultimate goal is to make dialogue a way of life; a way of engaging with the problems and the prospects of the global village. It is to dethrone the god of war and violence, and to consecrate the goddess of conversation—the conversation that takes place in the ultimate personal depth. Dialogue is a pilgrimage to depth in an age of superficiality.

We must dialogue not only because the global community is sitting over a likely holocaust, but we must converse—even more importantly—because we are human beings, and dialogue is the nourishment of our humanity. Our very survival as a sane species depends on it. But we need to survive as human beings. What does it profit us when we survive at the cost of our humanity? Overpowering violence may, theoretically, enable some people to survive. But only dialogue can safeguard at once the future and the nature of our species as a whole.

PART II

1

Religion and Spirituality: Swami Agnivesh in Conversation with Students from Clark Theological Seminary, Nagaland, India

Friends,

I invite you to join me for an inward journey, which is much different from the journey you undertook from Nagaland to Delhi.

I was born and brought up in the Hindu Brahmin tradition. Having lost my father at the age of four, I was brought up by my maternal grandfather, who was very compassionate. Along with him, I would worship all gods and goddesses, observing all rituals.

In my childhood, I had many difficult questions to ask about gods and goddesses, such as: 'Why has a god so many heads?', 'How does the god with three heads use the pillow when he goes to bed?', 'What is the real significance of one god looking like a monkey, another like an elephant and yet another like a lion?', etcetera. My elders were unable to give any satisfactory answers. Instead, they would say that these are handed down and followed through the ages, and one should not question them. So I literally believed that it must be so, because God was like that. There were stories and superstitions too, like a cat crossing my way would be considered inauspicious. Thus, even when I grew up, I was afraid of a cat crossing my way.

At the age of seventeen, I came across a movement called Arya Samaj. I started learning the Vedas and Upanishads through the interpretations given by an enlightened rebel, Swami Dayanand, who was poisoned to death in 1883 for his radical ideas.

My association with Arya Samaj gave me a different world view altogether. Most important among the things I learnt was the principle that one should not depend on somebody else, however great—not even the Vedas and Swami Dayanand himself—when it comes to the matter of searching for truth. He taught that God is within you, and so the first step is to start your journey within. Go inside to the very force that keeps you alive. There is something happening to you every moment, because of which you are alive. Life stops when breath stops. So your existence is dependent on breathing. You have been breathing all your life. It is your life thread. Forget about your religion, forget about your nationality and all the learning you have. Now you are trying to know yourself: 'Who am I?'

You have been breathing, but have you been breathing consciously, like, now I have to breathe in, now I have to breathe out—is that the way you breathe? If you were to breathe in and breathe out making a conscious effort, you will have time for nothing else. And even breathing would be impossible, for what will happen to your breathing when you go to sleep? So who has been breathing for you? What is the value of that breath? If I give you a glass of water or a cup of tea, you will thank me, but when you are breathing without your having to make any effort, somebody is breathing for you; you do not thank anybody. And breathing means oxygen getting inside and cleaning, renewing your whole body, which according to science has a hundred trillion cells. Can you imagine what a miracle this is! And all these one hundred trillion cells are being cleansed every moment. So when you meditate on yourself, you start meditating on your Creator, and then realize how compassionate the Creator is. You never say thank you for all this breathing happening. You take it for granted.

It takes time to evolve from within. For that, you need to go into silence every day: find a corner in your house, temple or church; relax completely, forgetting everything, including the body, stop thinking; and then ask yourself: 'Who am I? Who is breathing?' Observe the breath—inhaling and exhaling the air. Breathing is very subtle. Relax yourself completely, and for those ten minutes or fifteen minutes, forget the whole world, all business—just concentrate or be aware only of the breath, the highest gift of God, the most compassionate. Don't entertain any thoughts; relax and concentrate on breath. You will feel very relaxed, very peaceful inside—blissful, light. Try this simple thing. I am not asking you to pray the Hindu way, the Muslim way or the Christian way.

The Vedas and the Upanishads proclaim that God is nothing but the truth, all truth, and God is all love, compassion and justice. And the highest aim of all human life should be to commune with such a God daily and in every moment. God is there in every particle. Scientists are now talking of a subatomic particle. With the help of a large Hadron Collider, 27 kilometres in circumference, buried under the ground in Geneva, for the last several years they have been experimenting with what is holding together those subatomic particles. You can't see them with your naked eye. It was on 4 July 2011 that they found this new thing which they called dark energy. And when people insisted on a proper explanation, in a way that they could understand, scientists for the first time used a term 'god particle'.

The Vedas and other schools of philosophy have maintained that God is there in every particle of the universe. Science today has come very close to this. When we say it is some sort of energy, which is not visible to the naked eye, we know this in our hearts and minds—every day you feel some energy of truth, don't you? You feel some energy of love, you feel some energy of justice, compassion—each one of you feels that. That is God's energy.

And we create our own artificial gods, or incarnation of God, or somebody a son of God, daughter of God, or husband of God, or a prophet sent by God, who is Allah. Allah has already sent you and me. When he created us with consciousness, love, compassion and an urge for justice and truth, this is one of the highest creations of God. Discover yourself, and respect all men and women anywhere and everywhere. We are all great with all the potential to become the greatest of the great. Jesus of Nazareth was crucified at the age of thirty-three and he is no more. Similarly, Rama died, Krishna died and Gandhi died; Nelson Mandela died recently. They all had the potential. You have to realize your own potential in terms of your commitment to truth, compassion and justice. These are the divine attributes of God which each one of us has.

You should read all scriptures and study all religions; read everything—but liberate yourself from being narrowed down to something. You have to expand your awareness and embrace the whole of the universe, so that you are a tiny little universe yourself. Break all barriers. Transcend and transcend yourself also by being more and more selfless. Now, when you don't say 'thank you' for every breath, what is it that you should do? You should return God's compassion. Every moment demands that you make this universe a better place—by not polluting it, by not spreading violence and hatred—that is how you enter into God's paradigm. What is most material is: Is your circle of love expanding or contracting? If it is all the time 'my family', 'my husband', 'my children' and 'I am going to church every Sunday, or every day', you are not expanding. On the contrary, you are contracting.

Jesus is important for us because he extended his love to all of humanity. At the young age of thirty-three he sacrificed himself. Gandhi was great because he expanded his affinities. We celebrate these human beings because of their capacity to love beyond borders and barriers—their capacity to stand up for justice for all people: other people, not for themselves or a narrow small family—and their capacity to stand up for truth and pay the price.

Every human heart has the capacity to understand truth, whether the particular human being is highly educated or not. You should have more knowledge, but it is not just knowledge; your capacity to know the truth makes you divine.

All institutions—religious, social, political and economic—suffer from the disease of patriarchy. Because of man's purported superiority, many times we address God as a male *he*, not as a female *she*. Unconsciously or subconsciously, it is all male patriarchal domination that is reflected in our culture and institutions. That is why in religion particularly, they don't allow women to be popes, or even priests. Only jobs like being a sister, nun or some singing duty is assigned to them. The same is the case with the Shankaracharyas, the Dalai Lama, or any maulana. Our other institutions are not different. Take, for example, property ownership. You will find that 99.99 per cent of properties are registered in the name of men, not women. Nobody questions this; nobody wants to change it.

So one way of worshipping or relating or saying thank you to your God for every breath is to change this world: change this universe, change norms, pull down prejudices, remove the caste system, marry intertribal, inter-caste.

All prejudices or discriminations by birth boil down to economic paradigms, and defining who is rich and who is poor. Millions and millions of children are just born poor. Not just poor, they are born in bondage: they might have been born today or yesterday, and yet there is a debt burden hanging on them, because their parents had taken on loans and have not been able to repay them. I have dedicated my life to freeing poor people from this bondage. So once you realize who your God is and who you are, things begin to change.

Q: Swamiji, can you tell us about your adventurous journey from Calcutta to Haryana? You became the education minister in Haryana. Your own government threw you out because you stood up for truth. Then you continued your struggle against bonded labour and child labour.

A: At the age of seventeen I went to Calcutta for my college studies. I chose to go to Calcutta, because there was nobody to support me financially, and in Calcutta I could go to morning classes and work in the daytime to earn my living. That was my compulsion. However, it became a blessing. In Calcutta, I got associated with the Arya Samaj movement. Till then, I had thought the Vedas were some religious books. I came to realize then that they were books of knowledge like physics or chemistry, and had nothing to do with any religion.

In Calcutta, it so happened that St Xavier's college offered me a teaching job even before the result of my examination was declared. It was a prestigious offer I could not believe. All those years, I used to think that Christian missionaries were out to convert people and divide this beautiful country, because this is what I had been told by some top leaders who would address the Arya Samaj functions. But here was a Christian institution offering me a job spontaneously. And I was surprised. No one, including my mentor at that time, was prepared to believe me. It was only when I firmly told them that it was not a joke and that I had really got a job, one of them gave a friendly suggestion that I should dress like a college professor as it would be bad to appear in the class wearing khadi kurta, dhoti and a Gandhi cap which was my usual dress. I went to my friends to borrow, and succeeded in getting a a pair of trousers from one, a coat from another and finally a tie from a third. I was also given a short demo on how to put on a tie. So this way, I started my first day as a college teacher. That was in 1963. From 1963 to 1968, I taught.

In 1967, a small village in north Bengal, Naxalbari, gave birth to a new movement, which came to be known as the Naxalite movement. Poor landless people took up arms for their land rights and killed some of the landowners. The movement spread Maoist ideology, and very soon it spread to the streets of Calcutta. All the top bright students of Presidency College, Scottish Church College and my own college joined this movement, leaving their studies. They said, 'Chairman Mao is our Chairman; we will bring equality, we will bring revolution; revolution grows from the barrel of the gun; we will shoot down class enemies,' etcetera. I was fascinated that there was going to be a revolution, because the rich were exploiting the poor, and I could see every day that those who worked the hardest were the poorest, and those who didn't work and cheated were the richest. I thought I must also join this revolution. But they said if I wanted to join, I should 'take a gun and kill'. I couldn't indulge in violence. So, I thought, let me find an alternative.

I was very comfortable in Calcutta University, teaching postgraduate students economic development and corporate finance and practising in Calcutta High Court. So I was well placed in the worldly sense. But then there was a deep urge for justice: why are the poor, poor? And my religious people would tell me, 'Give some charity to those poor people!' But I would ask myself: In this country, who produces the food? It is these very people, the farmers. And why are they poor, why are they hungry? Who builds the houses, who bakes the bricks, who breaks the stones, who builds the buildings? And why don't they have buildings? If they grow food and they don't have food, something is basically wrong with the structure of things.

It is not enough that you do charity, and someone says you have a good conscience. You have to ask the basic question: 'Why are the poor, poor?' If it is because your caste system, economic system and political system are wrong, change them. Change through the gun? No, there is another way of changing. Then I decided to give up everything and leave it all behind. I was not married, and that left me free to make this decision. So I quietly took a train to Delhi and from there another to a Haryana village. There, I organized the poorest of the poor: farmers, bonded labourers, child labourers, brick kiln workers. All these movements and my activism since March 1968 you already know.

In 1968, I started my new life in spiritual activism,

which was rooted in my understanding of the Vedas and Upanishads. In the true spirit of the Vedas, I followed no religion or rituals. In this path, I met Swami Indravesh, who was barely three years older and yet had deep political insight with spiritual activism. Together, we launched a political party in 1970, based on the ideology of Vedic socialism. In this new life, I fought against the bonded labour and the child labour systems. I served in the United Nations in Geneva as chairperson of the UN Trust Fund on Contemporary Forms of Slavery. I am the founder and chairperson of the Bonded Labour Liberation Front and president of the World Council of Arya Samaj.

I fought against the practice of sati. A young seventeen-year-old widow was forced, in the name of sati, to immolate herself to death on the funeral pyre of her husband in 1987, in a village called Deorala in Rajasthan. In order to put pressure on the government and the obscurantist forces, we organized a march from Delhi to Deorala and walked for eighteen days in the fierce winter of 1987. This resulted in the enactment of a new law by Parliament: the Sati Prevention Act, 1987.

Similarly, Dalits were not allowed to enter the Nathdwara in Udaipur district. I fought against this, and had the temple opened for everybody. Through our movement, we had 176,000 bonded labourers freed and rehabilitated.

Q: It is such a great privilege for all of us to meet you and learn from you. It is just wonderful hearing from you. But as a Christian or as a Hindu, is scripture not important? Most importantly, how do we deal with an environment in which we live and the togetherness with which we live with our neighbour? Will you enlighten us with your wonderful wisdom? Coming back to places of worship, Christians go to church—and correct me if I am wrong or my question is immature—what is your view on the importance of places of worship? For Christians, who give importance to building churches where believers come together to worship despite caste or distinction, could you enlighten us with what you think on the importance of building places of worship?

A: Good question. You would better ask your ancestors what they used to do before they were converted to Christianity. Tribals practise the best form of worship: no temple, no church, no mosque. For them, nature is a place of worship. A mountain, a forest, a spring, the sun, the moon and the stars—these are what they consider their temple. There is more spirituality in a tribal community. They even have matriarchal traditions that are not in the so-called civilized communities.

Christianity is, after all, 2,000 years old, and what was the religion before that? Some would say Judaism. But that was there only in that particular area. For the whole of humanity, what was the religion? And we are not just 2,000 years old; we are millions of years old. If humanity could sustain without any organized religion for millions of years, why should we need a particular type of building for worship? We create these buildings, churches or temples, and kill each other in the name of our holy places, or religious places. We are the real temples. But we are killing each other, the 'God-created temple'—what a foolishness! How can you call a mosque a house of Allah? 'House of Allah' is the whole universe. How can you call a small place like this church a house of God? How can that be? The whole universe—and when you talk of the universe, find out from your science books what the size of your planet Earth is in this whole universe. Not even as little as a grain of sand in the whole scheme of the universe is your planet Earth. God is creating the universe. You are not relating to your God by creating a small place of worship. So I say your heart and mind are your real church, with love, compassion and truth—all of these. Gandhiji never went to a temple. He was a nice human being. And Jesus himself went to the synagogue only to fight against the so-called priests who were doing undesirable things in the name of religion or God. They were trading gods. He said, 'You cheats, get out.' They were angry and so he was crucified.

Why can't we all live in harmony? A Manipuri or a Naga, what is the difference? Why can't we fight the real enemy—alcohol and drugs? Let us join hands and say *no* to drugs, *no* to alcohol. Then it would be something worthwhile. But they quarrel in the name of tribes—Naga, Manipuri, this and that—leading to violence. The real issues are forgotten. Wherever church leaders stood up and stayed with the people, the church establishment pronounced them communists. There are rare exceptions though. In Latin America, there was a great archbishop whose name was Helder Camara. I quote him in my speeches. He said, 'When I give bread to the poor, they call me a saint, but when I ask why the poor do not have bread, they call me a communist.' And the Pope from Rome pronounced him a radical. When I talked of the Vedas and socialism, I was renounced as a communist and Marxist—although I was neither of these—because I asked the basic question: Why are the poor, poor?

If you really want to say 'thank you' to God in the morning, afternoon and evening, change the systemic structures which are anti-God and anti-creation. It is a murderous scheme of things, especially the rapacious arms industry. It must be banned completely. There should be no atom bombs and guns. The Bible you read dreams of a time when 'swords will be turned into ploughshares'. Then, how come the so-called Christian countries are filling the world with worse than swords? Don't you have a duty to demand that they be abandoned in favour of ploughshares when millions are dying of starvation? Love should be the weapon, even with those with whom we have differences. Alcohol and pornography are other big industries that are polluting the young minds today. They are destroying our family values and human values, and commodifying everything. We are not questioning them. Instead, we are questioning each other among the Hindu, Muslim and Christian communities. We are all commodities. Human relationships are all commodities. We are all consumers in the market, and the mantra is *consume*. We are condemned to consume. Consume the earth, consume the wholesomeness of nature. Consumerism is the new religion—not Christianity nor Hinduism. Desire is the new fever. And we are all worshipping false gods. False gods will necessarily divide. There is only one God for the whole universe. Unity of humankind is assured only when we are centred on that One Universal God: the Creator God.

Q: We are five people here from different religions: Christianity, Judaism and Islam. We want to prove that we can live together. Social cohesion in France is a bit complicated now. Living together is one thing, but doing something is different. While travelling, we try to meet people who are involved in interface. People whom we meet communicate and raise awareness. We have met more than 250 people—hopefully 500 by the end of our trip. We will use this as the raw material for research on interface around the world. It is too early to give conclusions. Is interface the means or an end? Interface, at least in Europe and France, hasn't been looked into much. What is tolerance for you, what is coexistence to you?

A: There are four Vedas, eleven Upanishads and eighteen Puranas. Nowhere in these books will you find a mention of the word 'Hindu'. Yet a large number of people call themselves Hindu. Where do you get this from? Hindu is not a religion. They say it is a way of life. Arya Samaj, to which I belong, is neither a religion nor a sect; it is a movement to bring closer all good people, right-thinking people, all over the world. We subscribe to Vedic teachings because they are universal and not sectarian. I must practise whatever is universal and good for the whole of mankind. I am very happy meeting my friends from other religions, like Hindus, Muslims, Christians and my black friends when I go to Africa.

What I got from Arya Samaj and from others are the three Ds. The first D is to Doubt. Always ask questions. Never accept anything on blind faith. The second D is to Debate in your mind; analyse. The third D is to Dissent if necessary. Do not accept something just because somebody in an influential position has told you to. That is also the teaching of the Buddha. Also, do not accept something because it is written in scripture or it has been going on for millions of years. Only if it is right in your own experience, follow that. That was Siddhartha Gautam Buddha's teaching. But the Buddha has also been made into a religion called Buddhism. Buddha never started a religion.

Q: It looks as if you are going beyond religion. Not only the religious dialogue; it is much more than that. Am I correct?

A: Yes. I question the very concept of religion. Religions as they are being practised or organized today in the world are all inherently sectarian. If you are a Hindu, you cannot be a Muslim or a Christian. Why live burdened by this narrow, dividing, sectarian identity? What is the difference between you and me? You will worship God with a different ritual, I will worship with a different ritual. Rituals and doctrines divide. God is the same. If only I can sincerely understand that my creator and your creator are the same, and that creator is truth and compassion, then I do not need these rituals; the dividing lines of temple, church and mosque. I do not need a maulvi, priest or pundit or a middleman. I will directly reach God, who is there in my heart and mind. So liberating God from the clutches of religion should be our spiritual mission. Religions have taken God hostage. God needs to be liberated. I am saying it in another sense. Christianity says God creates man in his image. But in actual practice, man creates God in his image. Because we are partial, we create a God who is partial. Redemption is possible only for believers. God is not partial. So we create all sorts of notions of God: gods, man, woman, prophet, this, that. So when we associate or make God sectarian instead of universal, we are destroying a very basic foundation. In Christianity, in Islam, in Hinduism, they do not relate themselves to God. They all relate themselves to middlemen like Rama, Krishna, Jesus or Muhammad. These middlemen who experienced God, are related to or worshipped more than the real god.

Q: I am a Christian, very orthodox. I am also a Bible teacher. The problem is that I have been believing in a God who is a personal God. I also believe Jesus is the embodiment of God. So I have difficulty in really accepting the way you explain God. How to overcome this? I have a book and I have a person who is God.

A: When I was brought up, I had multiple gods: Rama, Krishna, Vishnu and all of those images and idols, whereas you have only one Jesus. I had blind faith in what elders told me. When I joined the Arya Samaj, I questioned my own belief system. I asked: Is God universal or parochial? If God's creation is one integrated, whole universe—the sun and the moon and the stars and the whole solar system and beyond, and our planet Earth is like a grain of sand—who is sustaining this beautiful great universe? Only the creator God, and that can be only one, and that God is there in every particle of the universe. If you accept this definition of God being universal, God cannot have form. God is bound to be formless—that which is everywhere cannot be at one place by definition. God is there in the whole universe. Creation is a science, a law, and the beauty of God's creation is that this law cannot be broken anywhere. It is firm like a rock. The laws of the universe are very precise. Sitting here today, this day, you can calculate fifty million years from today, on what day, what hour, within a fraction of a second there would be an eclipse of the sun, and to what extent. You can calculate that and it will be exactly correct. This is called astronomy. We want that God, that force which is creating this law and sustaining this law, to be identified with some breaking of the laws: that He came to this earth without a father. God is unborn, unaging. Those who are born and those who die cannot be gods.

I have shared my perspective and I continuously question my earlier beliefs and try to evolve in my thinking on a daily basis. You should feel free to have your own perspective, a book and a personal God. But my friendly advice would be: keep questioning your belief system, keep evolving from within and without. Never be dogmatic.

I found it very rewarding to have been able to interact with you young minds.

2

Women's Empowerment: Swami Agnivesh in Conversation with Ms Maria von Welser, German Author, Television Journalist and Publicist

Q: Your contributions to women's causes are well known. Would you share some of your thoughts as to how you would like to go forward to achieve the goal in bringing about more equality between men and women?

A: India is such a huge country that it is always in turmoil. In fact, positive and negative things are happening simultaneously. Women need more empowerment—emotional, psychological and economic. The constitution or legislation alone will not help us realize the goal, because it is a huge social issue, having its root in the human psyche. In normal circumstances, the political establishment responds with yet another law, like in the case of domestic violence, or the Supreme Court's judgment in the Vishakha case for harassment in the workplace, or the recent legislation on rape.

Q: Could you elaborate, giving some examples and what should be done?
A: The first and foremost requirement is education and the upbringing of a girl child. But in the Indian context, I should start from the birth itself. We have this huge, abominable problem of female feticide in India—getting rid of the girl child before she is born. And contrary to popular belief, it is the well-to-do and the well-educated segment of society that resorts to this heinous crime more than the uneducated, illiterate or poor. The law has not been effective. To my mind, the most effective way of putting an end to this heinous practice is for the woman—the expectant mother herself— to take a firm stand and say *no* to any prenatal test. In the initial stages, it is likely to invite wrath from the insiders, who want to do the wrong. But let there be some resistance from the mother. As of now, even a little harsh word would make her melt and oblige. That should not be allowed to happen. In the event of extreme coercion, the mother should take the legal route to protect her

child by registering a complaint with the police. It is a question of changing one's mindset. Changes are happening, but at a snail's space. Spiritual masters, religious leaders, the priestly class and other social groups and the media all have important roles to play. All of them have to put their energy together and work in tandem.

The situation of the girl child is very poignant, because she is in her mother's womb. There can't be a safer place anywhere in the universe for the little child. And yet there she is being threatened, for no fault of her own, and the mother is not able to protect her own child. That is the height of haplessness.

On the legislation front, the law should provide for abortion only in exceptional cases: when there is a danger to the life of the expectant mother, or the conception itself was an outcome of a rape or some other rare and unforeseen circumstance. If it is the case of a selective abortion of a girl child, the law should provide for deterrent punishment for the guilty. The law as it exists today in India has many loopholes, and this has opened the floodgates for rampant abuse. The National Commission for Women (NCW), in its advisory role to the Government of India, owes it to the women of this country to strengthen the law to protect the girl child in the mother's womb.

Coming to the social aspect, women in India have traditionally remained a deprived lot in two important spheres. The first is education and the second is property rights. Good education has the highest potential for changing anybody's life for the better. At the same time, good education presupposes the need for good teachers. This is a gigantic challenge for a huge country like India. It requires political far-sightedness to invest in the creation and development of better citizens. Therefore, a lot remains to be done to bring good education to the doorsteps of poor people, so that a poor little girl is able to get it. It is also a matter of concern that many Indian women, even after getting quality higher education, remain in the domestic sphere—either of their own volition or because of social inhibitions—rendering all their education of no use, except for bringing up children.

Religion being an offshoot of society, its mindset is essentially patriarchal. Look at the way we address God in our common parlance. We always use the word *'he'* for God and not *'she'*. Everything is in terms of 'he'—man. In India, some in the Hindu religion believe in and worship goddesses like Maa Durga, Maa Saraswati, etcetera. This has very great significance. Mother is the embodiment of love and inclusiveness. Every living being is born out of a mother's womb. Mother's love is real and divine. Ignorant of this truth—deep in the mindset of man—a woman is accorded a second-class citizenship.

Dowry is another social evil in India that has been largely responsible for female feticide. In the absence of education and economic independence, a girl child has been looked upon as a liability. Although the law is gender neutral, women's property rights are not recognized. It is a clear case of not implementing what is there in the law. There has to be a social recognition that a woman is an equal partner to a man, which is still a difficult pill for a patriarchal society to swallow.

Q: So, do you mean that unless women become strong—if they don't take out rallies, if they don't talk loud and clear—nothing would happen?
A: Women mostly suffer because of their culture of silence. The way of their upbringing itself is responsible for this to a large extent. On the emotional front too in general, a woman gets a stepmotherly treatment from her own mother. Whenever a little girl protests at her brother, the mother chides her. When she speaks loudly, she is told not to shout, not to speak loudly. So, even at home, there is a different set of rules for girls. They

are told not to even sneeze. This is not only bad for their physical and psychological health, but also for their empowerment. In literature there is a very celebrated woman poet in our country. Her name is Subhadra Kumari Chauhan. Her most notable poetry in Hindi is about a woman warrior, the queen of Jhansi, Jhansi ki Rani Lakshmibhai. The poem is taught all over the country. In that poem, she talks about the fighting spirit of the queen of Jhansi. The poem goes like this:

Bundele har bolo ke muh hamne suni kahani thi.
Khub ladi mardani voh to Jhansi vali rani thi.

Everybody knows it; it is a popular poem. But there is an issue with the poem which normally people don't understand at all. It says 'khub ladi mardani'—which means she fought like a man. 'Mardani' means like a man. I say, why not 'zanani', which means like a woman? It is believed that only when you are like a man, you can fight. A woman is by culture not supposed to fight.

Q: Is there a chance to get men on the side of women for a better life? If women are empowered, it brings them a better life.

A: I have met women's representatives from the

world over, who have quite often brought up the idea of getting men on the side of women for their empowerment, which in turn leads to a better life. There is no dearth of men coming on the side of women for women's empowerment. In my opinion, it should start from the early childhood education itself—respect for the other should be inculcated among boys.

Q: But what could happen in the future? You have missing girls, millions of girls. Men are raping, kidnapping and trafficking women. These girls in their early teens—thirteen to fourteen years of age—are totally innocent.
A: It is a huge problem that we have—missing girls in the millions. I fail to understand why, in spite of a deterrent law—like the one we have had recently put in place—nobody is questioning the flesh trade, which is thriving. Girls are being trafficked from across the borders of Nepal, Bangladesh and the tribal areas and are being forced into prostitution. Does anybody bother to understand that 90 per cent or more of these girls are not voluntarily going into this profession? And yet the administration is simply taking it as something normal, and police and other officials, including judges and the political class, turn a blind eye. So if rape is a crime, here is a case of gang rape every day. Poor little girls are being gang-

raped in brothels every day. Nobody raises questions about the identity of those rapists. The whole issue is being swept under the carpet.

While returning from Sati Yatra in December 1987, on the way we encountered some women working in the fields, with whom we entered into a conversation. I asked them what they do when a male child is born. I could see everybody's face light up, and they said, 'Yes, we celebrate.' Then I asked them what they do when a girl child is born. There was no answer. Some said that they have the custom of breaking old earthen pots. When I pointed out that this is done when somebody dies, and it is a sign of mourning and not of celebration, the answer was that it is customary. Why is there no celebration on the birth of a girl child? Nobody questions these customs.

Returning from the yatra, we noticed so many clinics all around Delhi which carried out prenatal tests. We protested against those clinics and tried to build up a movement demanding legislation like that which we had in Bombay. There was no Central legislation. Eventually, the government got down to work and passed the PNDT Act in 1994 (the Pre-Conception and Pre-Natal Diagnostic Techniques Act, 1994). Still, there was no let-up in the fall of the female population. According to the

1991 census, about five million girls were missing. Now the figure stands at fifty million. The number is going up. There has to be a people's movement, so that the message goes down to the masses on this sordid picture, and enforcement of law begins on a serious note.

Q: So you have to rally again?
A: We took out a long march from the western part of Gujarat on a Diwali day, 1 November 2005, against female feticide. It was a fifteen-day-long march on vehicles, from a place called Tankara, the birthplace of Swami Dayanand. The good thing was that all religious leaders participated. The then health minister, Anbumani Ramadoss, represented the government. The media also rose to the occasion, which helped to create the kind of awareness that is essential for this sort of huge social cause. Many women-friendly schemes were initiated by the government and other voluntary organizations as a follow-up measure. It looked as if we were nearing a solution to many of the women's problems. In India, quite often, the situation is like firefighting. Only in the wake of a big disaster or a hue and cry, do the government and people wake up from their usual deep slumber.

Q: Are you now planning a new rally for changing the mood of the country for the good of women?
A: When I was in the Vatican immediately after 9/11, Pope John Paul II invited me to what they called a Prayer for Peace. 9/11 took place in 2001, and we were in the Vatican on 21 January 2002. Around 350 top religious leaders from all over the world had gathered in the auditorium of the Vatican. Eight persons had been chosen to speak, of which I happened to be one. I was seated next to Prince Hassan bin Talal of Jordan. When my turn came, I got up and addressed the audience—deliberately: 'My dear sisters and brothers', and then paused, 'Where are my sisters?' It was a big jolt to the entire religious gathering. Everybody looked at each other and wondered at what this Swami from India was trying to convey. I continued, 'Have we come here to meditate for peace? Let me tell you, my friends: as long as we do not give women of the world an equal place in the world of religion, there can be no peace in the world.' There was a big round of applause.

Five years later, the king of Saudi Arabia invited me to Madrid, Spain, and the situation was no different. This was for the Interfaith Dialogue Conference of the Muslim World League, a passionate project of the late King Abdullah bin Abdul Aziz Al Saud of Saudi Arabia. All sessions were being conducted by religious leaders—but all were men. From the audience, I got up on a point of order and asked, why are women not being allowed to be speakers? It had a salutary effect. In the very next session, they invited a well-educated Muslim woman to be one of the speakers. When she rose to speak, there was a huge applause. I was also congratulated.

Things are changing, even in Saudi Arabia. In KAICIID (King Abdulla International Centre for Inter-religious and Intercultural Dialogue)—a new initiative by King Abdullah of Saudi Arabia, headquartered in Vienna, of which I am one of the board members—there is one Alla Nasief, a woman from Saudi Arabia, who is doing very well as the chief of staff. A Buddhist woman from Tokyo, Japan, is on the board. In a sharp departure from the past, some of our board members are now coming with their wives for board meetings.

I feel India is a place where the challenges as well as opportunities are more because of poverty, socio-economic inequality and the parliamentary system of democratic functioning. Organized religions have a very strong presence in India, but they are unable to come up with anything tangible. Arya Samaj has a number of women priests. It is a reform movement for all religions, particularly Hindus. All religions put together, the picture is disappointing. While the secular, non-religious or political movements are doing better in spirituality, those who claim to be religious and spiritual are lagging behind. In my opinion, more than others, the United Nations and secular constitutions have done more in reclaiming the essence of spirituality. There is no attempt to redefine scriptures.

Q: Am I right in feeling that you are slightly depressed about the overall state of affairs?

A: It is depressing for me to find that social movements undertaken by us are not followed up in earnest by all sections of society. The media also fails to stay focused, and moves on after highlighting an event here and an event there. I am sure if we succeed in mobilizing thousands of women on the streets, the media will have no option but to take note of it. Even when we were fighting for 33 per cent women's reservation in parliament and state assemblies, I used to ask myself: Why do women themselves not come out in numbers?

Q: Do you think it is in some way our own fault?

A: What I feel is that women activists themselves and their movements have to be far stronger than what they are today.

Q: Don't you think there has to be a solution for women?
A: Yes, a solution in terms of some social action. We need to identify such women and give them moral and other support. Nobody from outside can empower a girl if she herself does not feel that she must have more power.

In order to defend one's own country, there is a huge budget. A large military is being trained; all sorts of armaments are mobilized from all over the world in order to defend its borders. In proportion to that, it is not even 0.01 per cent that we spend on empowering women in our country, where they fight daily battles. From the womb to the tomb, women's lives are full of struggles against inequalities, inequities—injustices for the redressal of which there is no institutional framework. Existing mechanisms are not enough to really empower women, and in order to see that coming true in our own lifetime, we need to work with some urgency.

Q: How can we make it happen?
A: UN organizations like UNICEF should take the lead. Children include women. Alternatively, there can be initiatives through other outfits of the UN. Constant interaction with the government on behalf of the UN would build up the required

pressure. The Beijing Declaration 1995, in the UN's fourth World Conference on Women, particularly on CEDAW (Convention on the Elimination of All forms of Discrimination against Women), was a very powerful one. The UN should itself prioritize the implementation of CEDAW and set up a decentralized body in every nook and corner of our world, and equip women with the latest communication technology such as women's community radio.

3

Naxalism in India—an Overview: An Interaction between Swami Agnivesh and Ms Alison Cameron of Melbourne, Australia

Q: Swamiji, could you share your thoughts on the emergence of Naxalism in India and how it impacted your life and initial days of social activism?

A: Naxalism first raised its head in India way back in 1966–67, when there was one-party rule both at the Centre and the states and much exploitation in the country. People, particularly the poor and marginalized, were disillusioned that there was no alternative to the Congress party. The movement started in a small village called Naxalbari in north Bengal, for implementing land reforms when there was a problem of too much landownership with one section of society, and too much landlessness for the poor and the peasants. Young men and women took up arms to redress the problem. In their bid to redistribute land to the landless labourers, the armed youth resorted to the killing of some landlords, police personnel and some administrative officers. This was a new development in our country, where the administrative system has been corrupt, inefficient, anti-people and anti-poor. The movement was influenced by what was known as Maoism. It started spreading to many parts of West Bengal. In those days, I was teaching in St Xaviers College, Calcutta, and I found the movement spreading fast and reaching the corridors of prestigious colleges like Presidency College, Scottish Church College, etcetera. Leading newspapers of the time, such as *The Statesman*, carried editorials suggesting that the new movement was going to change the very face of politics. Students and the teaching community were all excited by the new political adventure, and so was I. However, I was not quite comfortable with some of their postulates like 'Chairman Mao is our Chairman' and their reference to Mao's red book for solutions to all our problems. They talked of Marxism, Leninism and Mao's thoughts, and looked very radical among the leftists or communists and Marxists. Young men and women were taking up arms to fight injustice.

I was always against people taking up arms and killing in the name of justice. Rather, it was a violent and undemocratic movement, and particularly in a country like India, which has a profound Constitution and constitutional guarantees on human rights, it was bound to be counterproductive. Not knowing much about the differences between Marxism, Leninism and Maoist thought, but still fascinated by a new chapter of leftist extremism, I found myself challenged. To me, the fundamental question was: What is the answer when the constitutional mandate is not being implemented? When laws made by parliament and state legislatures are not being enforced, and the police, and the whole system, is corrupt to the core, what do you do? I knew that what I was doing then—teaching business management to children from rich families, or practising law under a leading lawyer who subsequently became Chief Justice of the Supreme Court of India—was not the real answer to those basic questions. At the same time, my inability to do anything made me feel guilty. Therefore, I took a decision to leave a prestigious job in Calcutta and quietly moved over to the other side of India, west of Delhi, that is, Haryana. This was in the year 1967.

In Haryana, I met a young ascetic, Indradev Medharti of a gurukul; he became Swami Indravesh later on. This young man impressed me with his political thoughts. He spoke to me about organizing the people of Haryana on the lines of the Arya Samaj in such a way that we could take political power in our hands, ushering in an era of Vedic culture, which would be a political manifestation of Arya Samaj. The idea was to resuscitate Arya Samaj—which was in any case dying—get closer to the people, the poorest of the poor, and organize them for political power. It was very tempting, because whatever little I knew of Maoist literature was corroborated by the talk of this young ascetic, that is, surrounding the cities with villages and then the village community moving into the city and taking over the reins of power. Since Haryana was located on all the three sides of Delhi, we thought it was ideally placed to make the surrounding villages our base area to work for the farmers, labourers and the poor, with a view to seizing power in Haryana. I started working with Indradev Medharti. Soon our tribe expanded to many more, who were ready to dedicate their lives to work for a change in the political system—leaving their jobs and life's other commitments behind.

Q: How did you manage to entice them into that change?

A: First of all, Swami Indravesh's own life was enticing me—if he could do it, why not I? And if he and I could do it, why not others? This was a multiplying factor for most of us. Young people got to know each other—all were pro-change. And the very thought that we could form a political entity, and could well be an alternative to the monolith Congress rule in the Centre and the state, was an attraction for people. Moreover, when we talked of political change, we just did not confine ourselves to political manoeuvring, etcetera. We questioned all unethical, immoral and corrupt practices, and talked of nothing less than a moral regeneration, that is, an Arya Rashtra, which meant a noble, value-based nation in politics. Our first movement was against alcoholism and the liquor policy of the then Government of Haryana, headed by Chief Minister Bansi Lal, who was dreaded like a dictator. Haryana was a newly carved-out state from Punjab, and Bansi Lal, in his zeal to modernize and develop the state and usher in an era of green revolution, needed huge sums of money for building roads and bringing electricity to every village. In order to carry out his dream formula of modernization, he thought that the best way was to open more liquor outlets and auction them to garner requisite funds.

Q. So that is the initial phase of your social activism. Could you reflect more on the first few years of the Naxal phenomenon and how it influenced your journey in social activism?

A: That earlier phase of Naxalism and Maoism I was describing had fascinated me. And though I went in a different way, I joined hands with Swami Indravesh, who was working for Vedic socialism—which was about radical ideas in the ownership of land and other means of production, challenging the law of inheritance, community ownership of means of production. However, some of our radical political friends held the view that in no way could we have a society where the means of production could be taken over by the state and redistributed in favour of the poor. Nevertheless, we were struck with the zeal for change.

Unfortunately, around that time in the late 1960s or early 1970s, we also learnt that the Naxal movement, which had by then taken root in West Bengal and other parts of eastern India, was heavily put down by the then chief minister of West Bengal, Siddhartha Shankar Ray. He unleashed a reign of terror against the young Maoist men and women. He crushed the movement in every possible way, killing many in fake encounters. Within a few years, everybody thought the movement was gone, though it was spreading in some other parts of India, including Punjab. However, it is noteworthy that there was no trace of it either in Haryana or in western Uttar Pradesh. This gave a fillip to our hope that we might be able to come up with the new alternative in Haryana, in a peaceful and democratic manner.

Meanwhile, the Naxal movement—though crushed and its leaders either arrested, jailed or even done to death in fake encounters and the like—did not completely die down. It started manifesting in the form of some other movements. It was in the first half of the 1970s. A young man by the name of Shankar Guha Niyogi—who was also born in a village near Naxalbari—after doing a bachelor's degree in science, became influenced by the ideology of Maoism / Naxalism, moved over to Calcutta, and from there he sneaked into present-day Chhattisgarh in central India to create a base in the tribal belt. There, he organized the iron ore mine workers, who were being subjected to all sorts of inhuman exploitations. In a unique way of identifying himself with the local people, he married a mine worker's daughter by the name of Asha, and built his own little hutment in the midst of the labourers' homes in a small village called Dalli Rajhara. He fully identified with the hopes, aspirations and the nitty-gritty of life in the tribal belt. His idealism took him to the extent of joining the workforce as a labourer himself. Alas, in the process, he left some of those approaches or ideas of Naxalism, and got more and more drawn towards the Gandhian philosophy of non-violence and social reforms. This had its own repercussions. Some of his own comrades thought he was a risk to the movement and wanted to get rid of him. They called him a revisionist. And for some reason, he was in jail for a while. In jail, he happened to read one of my essays published in a leading weekly magazine, *Dharma Yug*. It was a long article on how to integrate culture and spirituality with the process of political change. The title was 'Dharma ka diya aur kranti ki bati' (The lamp of spirituality with the wick of revolution). After reading it, he wanted to meet me. I also used to read some of his reports about his unique way of organizing labour, and was keen to meet him. It was finally around 1977–78 that we were able to meet, when he was released from jail. There was a lot in common between us, and we became good friends. After the meeting, he used to invite me for all major functions in his area. The fact that I was also brought up in the Chhattisgarh region was an advantage, in that I was able to speak in the local dialect fluently in public meetings. Responses from the people were overwhelming. For them, it was a curious case of a swami talking of radical socio-economic politics, and this was a good enough cocktail for them.

All said and done, it was taken that Naxalism, as it had erupted in the first phase, was over, but soon we heard about some regrouping in the state of Andhra Pradesh, in the name of People's War Group. The issues and chain of events with the new outfits were once again the same as Naxalism—land rights issues, taking up arms for resolving them, getting caught; killing and getting killed. This was in the early 1980s, but I was nowhere close to any of these groups, except in that some of their cultural outfits used to invite me to speak from their forums. I would go and use their platforms to speak against social and economic disparities, human rights, the bonded labour system, and above all, exploitation. Again, the response from people was very encouraging.

The heartland of Maoism has been the tribal belt of central India. From northern Bengal it penetrated into Orissa, Jharkhand, Bihar, Chhattisgarh, Maharashtra and Andhra Pradesh. With more repression and exploitation, more and more tribal people joined the Maoists' ranks. Tribals were being denied their forest rights and land rights. Their culture was being invaded in the name of so-called development. The state machinery itself was corrupt. All of this ensured more support of the people to the Maoists. They became a threat to the state and political parties. Ironically, Maoists specially targeted the Marxist party who ruled West Bengal, so much so that the Marxists would rue the fact that some of their own ideological bedfellows were now their biggest enemies. Maoists would resort to guerrilla tactics and kill some of the activists of the Commonist Party of India (Marxist) (CPI-M). The CPI-M activists were also trying to use their new-found political power to suppress political dissent in villages, and were also not sincere in implementing laws. Thus, there was a running battle between the Maoists and the Marxists. It lasted for several years.

Q. Could I now take you to Delhi in the present time and the work you have been doing with Maoists in trying to procure some sense of peace and dialogue with the government?

A. The former prime minister of India, Dr Manmohan Singh, has been crying hoarse that Maoism/Naxalism is the single biggest threat to India's internal security. He admitted that Maoists had a growing appeal among the tribals, rural poor, intelligentsia and youth; and dealing with Naxalism requires a holistic approach, as it cannot be treated as a mere law and order problem. State governments have been demanding more force, more arms and training to fight the menace. Many a time, the striking force of Maoists proved to be more lethal than that of the government's paramilitary forces. Paramilitary forces would not know the terrain—thick forests in mountainous regions—and the Maoists knew how and where to lay mines on the roads and blow up their vehicles. And so on and so forth.

The biggest Maoist strike since 1967 took place on 6 April 2010, in the forest region of Dantewada in the state of Chhattisgarh, in which seventy-six Central Reserve Police Force (CRPF) men were killed in an ambush. The whole state machinery was taken aback, as all their preparations could not face up to the crisis. It appeared as if the government was going to embark on a major operation. They started mobilizing more paramilitary forces with more guns and other weapons. There were media reports suggesting that an 'Operation Green Hunt' was about to be launched to eliminate the Maoists.

To avert a major crisis, we undertook a march from Raipur to Dantewada just a month after the 6 April massacre. On 5 May, we gathered in the city of Raipur, held a press conference followed by a public meeting the next morning, and marched from the Gandhi statue in Raipur. We said 'gun for gun, bullet for bullet' was no answer to India's nagging problems of poverty, disparity and exploitation.

Therefore, there was an urgent need for cessation of hostilities from both sides. Operation Green Hunt had to stop, and Maoists, instead of taking to armed revolution, had to sit down with the government at the dialogue table and thrash it out. I gave out a slogan which was earlier coined by Nirmala Deshpande, who used to say in the context of Kashmir and other places: 'Goli se nahi, boli se' (not by bullets, but through dialogue). But there were some political hardliners in the government who were opposed to the idea of dialogue, and they wanted to crush the Maoists completely.

On my return to Delhi after the march, I got a letter from the then home minister P. Chidambaram, congratulating me for the march and thanking me for all I had said about the peace process and dialogue. The letter also spelt out a five-point approach to invite the Maoists for dialogue. Such offers for dialogue were extended to the Maoists in the past too, provided they abjured violence for seventy-two hours. But this time, it looked different, because it was for the first time that a letter for a peace proposal was issued duly signed by the home minister of India, sealed in an envelope and marked confidential. I was happy that the home minister had finally recognized our efforts, and it was time we engaged in peaceful dialogue in a serious manner.

However, I was handicapped in not being able to share the contents of the letter with my friends—intellectuals and professors who were closer to the Maoists—as it was marked 'confidential'. Therefore, they were not fully convinced.

A few days later I found, to my surprise, that in an interview with one of the television channels, the home minister himself made the contents of his letter public. I took the home minister's permission and shared a copy of the letter with people who I believed were intermediaries for Maoists. The letter was sent to the Maoist Central Committee in their hideouts. Lo and behold, beyond all our expectations, a reply signed by their spokesperson, Mr Azad, on behalf of the Central Committee, was given to me. I could very well see the sincerity on the part of the Maoist party leadership and their readiness for a dialogue, provided there was a mutual ceasefire. Their demands included, among other things: lifting the ban on their party and releasing their political prisoners. However, the reply fell short of a commitment to abjur violence for seventy-two hours and then joining the dialogue process. In the letter, they also criticized the Central home minister's posture—on the one hand inviting them for dialogue, and on the other mobilizing the army and air force to crush them. However, I saw a lot of material in that letter to take the next step, and met the home minister again and again. He told me not to trust the Maoists and read too much into their reply, as they are all for overthrowing the state through violence. After making a fair assessment of what is in the minds of the government and the Maoists, I was prevailed upon by some of my very close friends that I myself should suggest a date for a ceasefire, instead of looking to the government or the Maoists to declare a date. Accordingly, I suggested three dates to the Maoist leadership and asked them to agree to one of the dates and convey it quietly to me, so that I could in turn convey it quietly to the government. Eventually, a seventy-two-hour period of cessation of violence would take place, and that would be the ideal situation for a mutual ceasefire agreement to be signed and implemented simultaneously.

Q. How do you continue to maintain that something positive can happen?

A. Well, I know their intentions. Government knows full well that through the sheer use of military or paramilitary force, they cannot put down the people's uprising. It is not just the hard-core Maoists. The tribals are giving them a lot of support. They are joining their ranks. Maoists also know that however romantic or committed they might be about a Mao-style or Chinese revolution, in this age of modern technology and warfare, a nation state like India cannot be overrun. Therefore, I think, once they get an opportunity and the ban is lifted, they will come above ground and would work for mobilizing people for political purposes.

Q. Would you say that even if the government knows that people's movements cannot be put down forever by using sheer force, are there some other reasons for using force?
A: Of course they are doing it for political gain; take for example, the criticism of the home minister by his own colleagues for being soft on Maoists by inviting them for talks, etcetera. And some of his other hawkish advisors were also not in favour of dialogue, but this gentleman home minister was sticking to his guns and saying, 'No, I have made this offer and I am going to stand by it, but it has to be on the lines suggested by the government.'

Q. He made the offer by calling them liars to their face, so has he been serious in his offer?
A. Yes, whatever be their inner motives, I was intent taking both the government and the Maoists at their face value, because violence for violence is not the answer at all. One day, they have to see reason and come to the talking table. The Indian

government had in 2009 announced an integrated action plan as a nationwide initiative to deal with the Naxalite problem. It was with the twin objectives of providing funding for grass-roots economic development projects in the Naxal-affected areas and increasing police funding for better containment of the Naxal influence.

Q. So you believe in the innocence beyond all of the egos and other complexities of the issue?

A. The exigencies and imperatives of the situation, on both sides, would also take them in the same direction. Whenever Maoists kill civilians, they get flak from the people and media. They cannot espouse reckless violence. Their own sympathizers are quite wary about this. Very recently, some of their front outfits removed fish plates from the railway track, resulting in the derailment of a train going from Calcutta to Bombay, killing nearly 150 people. The needle of suspicion was on the Maoists, but they denied having any connection with the incident. They are aware that once they are seen as targeting innocent people, they would be looked upon as terrorists, which is the last thing they want. Therefore, they condemned the incident and demanded an inquiry. An inquiry was ordered and the report is awaited.

4

A Critique of Selective Western Interventions and the World Trade Organization

Q: Do you fear outside commitment and intervention in the field of bonded labour and child labour? There is a debate vis-à-vis the World Trade Organization (WTO) about the Rugmark Foundation and its initiatives. What are your views in this respect?

A: At the initial stage, whenever there was any solidarity expressed by the foreign media or by the foreign powers or the foreign trade unions, we found strength—we found some welcome signs in that. But over the years, we have become very sceptical and suspicious about the motives behind some of these steps taken by the foreign powers. When the General Agreement on Tariffs and Trade (GATT) was being authenticated in Marrakesh in Morocco around 1993–94, the USA and France came out with a shrill orchestration of a new clause in the WTO, and they said that there should be a 'social clause'. And by 'social clause', they meant that child labour and forced labour should be the top priority of the social clause, meaning thereby that whatever is being produced directly or indirectly with child labour and forced labour, should not form part of world trade. It means that countries which have this endemic problem should not be allowed to export anything, or at least not products which have been manufactured with child labour or forced labour. In India, as per the Supreme Court's definition, a vast majority of the labour force is still languishing under conditions of bonded labour and bonded child labour. We came out with the exact figures at various national and international seminars, mentioning and accepting that as per the law and as per the definition, anyone who is being denied a minimum wage as statutorily fixed by the state governments is a bonded labourer. Child labour, in general, is not entitled to any minimum wage whatsoever. In fact, child labour is employed so that the employer does not have to pay minimum wages to adult labourers; hence the preference for child labour. So not only are the child labourers being denied minimum wages, but their basic right to education—which the Supreme Court has defined as their right to life and therefore a fundamental right—is also being violated. If the social clause were to be applied to our Indian situation, I am sure the country could not export even a blade of grass, a grain of wheat, a leaf of tea, a piece of granite, carpet, bangle, matchbox, leather goods, textiles—nothing of this sort—because of direct or indirect involvement of the unorganized labour force. There are approximately 450 million people languishing in conditions of bonded labour and forced labour, besides the fifty million children who are in conditions of bonded child labour. The total labour strength therefore oscillates at around 500 million. Therefore, nearly every third Indian today is in a condition of one or the other forms of forced labour. This is a very tragic comment on our country's situation.

But the way the powers behind the WTO want to solve this problem of bonded labour and child labour is not proper, and we suspect that the real motive behind the social clause has been protectionism. The developed countries of the West want free mobility of their capital so much that now they are debating whether to also impose the multilateral investment agreement on developing countries. Member countries of the Organization for Economic Cooperation and Development (OECD) have already seen it through. Now, they will bring it to the WTO. So all sorts of attempts are being made by the developed countries and their multinational corporations—who are the main players in this whole regime of the WTO—to see that their capital has free access to the markets of the developing countries. But they want to deny others access to their technology in the name of intellectual property rights and patent laws, etcetera. They are definitely hell-bent on denying free access of labour to the markets of developed countries, so much so that in recent years the immigration laws of the developed countries have been made more and more stringent. I may be excused if I perceive an element of racism in some of these immigration laws, and the fortress-like walls which have been raised in recent years. Even asylum laws in the developed countries are being tightened; freedom is being curtailed.

The West has not been able to come out clean in their championing of the human rights of poor and downtrodden child labourers or forced labourers. Instead of doing something radical about this situation—which prevails not just in India but also in Pakistan, Nepal, Bangladesh, Sri Lanka, Thailand and the Philippines, and in most of the countries of Africa and Latin America—instead of trying to find a global solution to a situation where the whole world is divided into 'haves' and 'have-nots', and where the main reasons for the perpetuation of the problems of bonded labour and child labour are not just trade relations, the developed countries are seeking to take this issue out of its context. Some basic changes in the world economy are required. Those questions are not being raised or debated properly. The developed countries are shirking their ethical, moral and political responsibilities deliberately, and are trying to have their own way in every matter which concerns their commerce, trade, industry and profit. This situation demands a serious review, and the place where the problems originate should be blamed and taken to task. Many of us—not only social activists but also serious economists the world over—have come to the conclusion that most of the violations taking place today in Third World economies have their origin in the First World in trade and commerce. I accuse, therefore, the Western powers of hoodwinking the poorer countries, politically as well as economically, and their insincerity is writ large. They don't want to grasp the problem and solve it once and for all. They are playing truant with the problem. They are trying to run with the hare and hunt with the hounds. It is a double-standard game, and therefore I don't trust even the Western media, which initially I thought was doing a great service by highlighting the plight of child labour and bonded labour in my country. I may be wrong, but I have my reasons, and I am glad that most of my country's trade unions—even political leaders and other NGOs and social action groups—share this particular perspective about the dominant Western intervention in matters of bonded labour and child labour.

Q. How do you assess the efforts of the so-called 'Rugmark label', which was originally initiated with help from the German Technical Agency (GTA)? How do you assess, in a second step, the 'Global March', which took place in early 1998? Would you say that it really helps the cause of committed work?

A: In this respect again, we were very enthusiastic when the idea was raised about 'Rugmark'-labelled carpets, which would have then had very good access to Western markets and would have been able to solve the problem of child labour, at least in the carpet industry. But after the initial enthusiasm died down, we found that there were certain other motives, and we started questioning a very discriminatory response of the Western countries—particularly that of the German government, the German parliament and German trade and industry—about the problem of child labour in my country. Rugmark was essentially an initiative of the Indo-German Export Promotion Project (IGEP). We earlier thought that the consumer action groups in the West and in Germany were taking the initiative, but much later we got to know that it was the German government which had largely funded the IGEP to bring about the Rugmark Foundation. When we came to know about this, we grew a little suspicious. Then came the second stage, when my colleague, Kailash Satyarthi, drifted away from the mainstream of Bandhua Mukti Morcha (BMM). Soon, he started barging in on the South Asian Coalition on Child Servitude (SACCS), which was lying defunct. Surprisingly, the vested interests started projecting him as the champion of the cause of child labour in India, and thereafter honours were heaped on him.

In the area of Rugmark Foundation, all my arguments with him, about his status in this organization being untenable, proved futile.

I held detailed discussions with Dr Dietrich Kebschull of IGEP on Rugmark, and he candidly conceded once that the way carpets are being woven in the informal sector in India, there is not a single shed, there is not a single factory where you can go and monitor the whole process of carpet weaving. In the whole process, right from acquiring and cleaning wool, supplying it and then getting carpets woven and applying the finishing touches, there are a number of sub-subcontractors. There is no way to monitor the process in rural areas, which are so far-flung that any number of inspectors cannot do complete and authentic monitoring. We are unable to reconcile this with the self-contradictory approach of advocating Rugmark labelling on carpets, assuring consumers that these are free from child labour.

It was against this backdrop that we became disturbed and we said that though Rugmark today might seem to be alluring and seem to fetch us a little market share in Germany and elsewhere, in the long run it will boomerang and will tell upon the credibility of not just the carpet industry, but the whole of the Indian economy. And all other things will be looked upon as suspect.

What will happen when consumers and other people realize that they have been duped—that they have been given a label which guarantees in its publicity that there has been no child labour involved whatsoever, but later find that there is a large input of child labour even in those carpets which bear the 'Rugmark label'? In the United States, I met one Mr

Pharis Harvey, who was with the Monitoring and Child Right Alliance based in Washington, very close to Capitol Hill. I had a long discussion with him. In the end, he also conceded that the label was not a 100 per cent genuine guarantee. But he baldly stated that in the United States, it is only the 100 per cent guarantee which sells; and nothing else. Therefore, he was more concerned with the marketing of the label, rather than with the authenticity or the genuineness, which was very unfortunate.

It was also unfortunate that the former German labour minister, Mr Norbert Blum, on his visit to India—perhaps due to a shortage of time—could not meet a cross section of the people involved with the child labour problem, and as such he could not study the issue enough to gain a real perspective. Based on the feedback provided to him, he expressed his advocacy of the Rugmark Foundation. This stance further raised doubts about the whole issue of the foundation.

The minister's stand of supporting and promoting Rugmark was very disturbing, and no sooner had this been done than it was picked up by Mr Robert Wright, the US labour secretary. He went a step further, and said that they were planning to extend Rugmark to textiles and also to some other goods. So this seems to be something which was very calculatedly planned and executed. Rugmark today, at least in the eyes of authentic social activists in this country, stands not just accused, but completely tarnished—and I don't know what its future will be. Certainly, people have started realizing that it is a fake label, and therefore the Western attempt to hoodwink us will not work. At least, it has not worked in our eyes, and we have become more suspicious of the motives of some of the initiatives which are coming from Western countries and being promoted by the Western media.

But our suspicions and our worst fears came true when we saw a huge march against child labour. This was termed a 'Global March', and again, the leadership was given to our erstwhile friend, Kailash Satyarthi, and his organization SACCS. The Western countries helped him to raise money: around two million US dollars or more was the initial contribution—maybe they doubled it subsequently. The International Labour Organization (ILO) decided to promote it because the International Confederation of Free Trade Unions (ICFTU) was supporting it as one of the dominant, important players. Therefore, the 'Global March' was first to assemble and converge in Brussels at the ICFTU headquarters, and only then proceed to Geneva, where the ILO was going to take up the whole question of the new convention on the intolerable forms of child labour.

We have seen through the game plan, and we think that the Western powers are out to sabotage the real onslaught against child labour exploitation. They are going to cash in on this whole situation. They are propping up leaders, they are propping up NGOs, they are propping up marches, so that they can, in the course of time, create a suitable atmosphere whereby they can bring in their 'social clause' to the WTO.

This was the ground which was being prepared through the Global March. The American celebrities who participated—and some of them were here in Delhi—were not shown child labour in agriculture or in the brick kilns or in the stone quarries; things which are not exported. They were straightaway taken to Jaipur. Kerry Kennedy was here; Bianca Jagger, the actress from America—these and other celebrities were straightaway flown to Jaipur to see child labour in the diamond polishing and diamond cutting industry. This made it very clear that the intention of the Global March was not to fight the child labour problem in its entirety, but just to highlight child labour in export-oriented industries. All said and done, the export-oriented industries constitute a very small percentage of the total child workforce. Nearly half of child labour is in agriculture; the other half is predominantly in industries or activities which are not at all exported. Only a small fraction is involved in export-oriented industries. But the West was interested in highlighting the Global March and export-oriented goods; and the question of the fundamental right to education of every child was never given a serious thought. The ILO exercise stands exposed. I was very sympathetic in working with the ILO, and the year before last I even participated in their annual meeting in Geneva. But now, I think that the ILO is playing to the same Western agenda, and its credentials are not very clear, not very clean. That is all I have to say about this Global March and the so-called Rugmark Foundation. The sooner it is exposed, the better it will be, not only for us in India, but also for the consumers in the West, who stand duped.

Q: It is sometimes easy to criticize. One has to be clear in the critical analysis, but what concrete steps would you propose and how do you see the perspectives of Indian children in the next decade?

A: You will excuse me if I say that I see the problem now in its entirety or rather, in a greater, broader perspective than what I used to see earlier. Now, it is not only the plight of the Indian child labourer which concerns me; it is child labour everywhere. Therefore, I want to raise this whole question. My perspective is now very clear: that the entire human civilization today stands accused.

All leaders, all opinion makers, all the elite of the world need to sit up and ask this small but most pertinent question: what have you done to our children on this planet? By ILO estimates, there are about 250 million children who have been denied their fundamental right to childhood, to education, to play and dream like normal children. Now, if there are 250 million such children all over the world—and the authentic estimates may come out later and may be higher than what the ILO had earlier estimated—it is the biggest slur on our civilization, our human culture. Therefore, all religious heads, all politicians, all trade union leaders and all such other well-meaning people the world over, should try to take upon themselves the responsibility to undo this greatest violation of human rights and human dignity. And since there must be some connection—as I said in the Indian context—a connection between the social dimensions and the economic dimensions in other countries must also be clearly recognized.

When I visited South Africa, I could see that among the street children and such other children who are still being exploited after independence, there are hardly any white children. Most children are black African children. It means that apartheid is still perpetuating itself. I found the same thing in the streets of Nairobi, Kenya, and I am sure that the same pertains to many other parts of our world. So all humanity now needs to take it up. When we are talking about globalization and the world being reduced to a global village, there is no reason why we cannot pool all our moral and material resources to combat this most pernicious problem facing humanity. If we cannot bring back the dreams of our children, we have no right to call ourselves civilized people. I think this is the biggest challenge. The challenge lies not only with politicians. Religious leaders are equally to be blamed: with all their temples, churches, mosques and gurudwaras and so many resources at their command. With their sway—their hold over the minds and hearts of the people—what have they done to combat this pernicious problem? They will need to ask themselves this question, and through this type of soul searching, I think we can overcome this problem. The ethical, moral and spiritual dimensions of this question are all the more important because children are the most beautiful gift of God on earth, and therefore tears in the eyes of the children, or their sullen, sunken faces, are telling statements on our ethical, moral and spiritual standards. In this way, I think, we need to address the problem. And this should be the perspective with which we take up the problem in the twenty-first century.

Acknowledgements

Forty-eight years ago, I came in contact with a young ascetic in Haryana who invited me to join him in the struggle to translate the teachings of Vedas as interpreted by the revolutionary Swami Dayanand into social reality. The call became so intense that I left my lecturership in St. Xavier's College, Kolkata, and, renouncing my worldly possessions, I proceeded to join him. Together we launched a people's struggle which landed us in jail where we both decided to embrace sanyas and plunge into a fierce struggle for socio-political justice on the lines of Vedic socialism. We later came to be known with our new identities: Swami Indravesh and Swami Agnivesh. Though only three years older than me, Swami Indravesh passed away seven years ago, leaving behind a legacy which I find difficult to shoulder. I would like to acknowledge my gratitude to the late Swami Indravesh and all those colleagues who left the world in the course of this struggle.

My deep involvement in electoral politics and the challenges I had to face as legislator and minister for education in Haryana were also part of my experiments with social spirituality as enshrined in the Vedas. Though I could not survive long in party politics because of my idealistic clash with entrenched vested interests, I plunged headlong to douse the communal flare-up that followed the assassination of Prime Minister Indira Gandhi. The ugly face of religion and the concomitant violence impelled me to take organized religions by their horns and dedicate my life to ushering in a universal spiritual ethos.

Soon after, I saw the competitive communal politics of the Congress party and the Bharatiya Janata Party which led to the demolition of Babri Mosque in Ayodhya. For years I campaigned against such communally charged politics and learnt a lot about how a ritual-ridden, dogmatic and superstitious religiosity can play havoc not only with people but also with religion and the very concept of God itself. I am indebted to all those villains and marauders who provoked me to revisit all religions and find how their practice has degenerated into a festering wound.

The Maliana massacre of forty-five Muslim young men by the Uttar Pradesh Police revealed the cancerous evil of communalism in the law and order machinery. We organized a march from Delhi to Meerut against this but to no avail. On the night of 22 January 1999, Christian missionary Graham Staines and his two sons were burnt alive deep in the Orissa forests. Our first-ever interfaith pilgrimage of compassion by train to Manoharpur was yet another episode in our fight against religious bigotry. Next was the 2002 Gujarat riots, a near genocide and another interfaith pilgrimage to Godhra, Baroda, Ahmedabad and Sabarmati. This gave enough material for me and Rev. Valson Thampu to co-author a book titled *The Harvest of Hate*. Years of collaboration with Valson Thampu provided a glimmer of hope that reinforced our mutual bonds which continue till date. I am deeply indebted to Rev. Valson Thampu for this spiritual partnership and for the insights he provided.

Marcel Rey, my friend in Zermatt, Switzerland, is another spiritual agent provocateur I am indebted to. He literally launched me into the tumultuous waters of international interreligious fora. From Amman in Jordan to Cape Town in South Africa, from Tokyo to Jakarta to New York and San Francisco, I virtually became, thanks to him, a jet-setting swami.

I learnt a lot but I tried to unlearn a lot also. It was at the Union Theological Seminary in NYC that Fr Thomas Keeting and Prof. Paul Knitter encouraged me to get my monograph 'Applied Spirituality' published by some internationally renowned publisher. I acknowledge their encouragement. And finally it was my friend and philosopher Dr Arun Shourie who introduced me to HarperCollins.

I acknowledge the editorial assistance of Prof. Vikas Baniwal and my colleague T.D. Thampi in finally seeing this through publication. T.D. Thampi's past experience with a renowned publisher helped me a lot. I owe all of them deep gratitude.